Night of the Living Dud

Mr. Satanism

Published by Inept Concepts, 2013.

While every precaution has been taken in the preparation of this book, the publisher assumes no responsibility for errors or omissions, or for damages resulting from the use of the information contained herein.

NIGHT OF THE LIVING DUD

First edition. June 7, 2013.

Copyright © 2013 Mr. Satanism.

ISBN: 979-8227626943

Written by Mr. Satanism.

Introduction

Chicks often ask me why guys like zombie movies so much, and the answer is simple: Guys like zombie movies because they secretly hope that any given one will be as good as the original *Dawn of the Dead* (1978). The answer to the follow-up question is equally obvious: Your boyfriend *is* an idiot who watches too many zombie movies, and I'll gladly fuck you while he's out of town, or even while he's downstairs if he's smaller than me and doesn't own a gun. Oops, sorry, wrong follow-up question. The *other* follow-up question they always ask is *Okay, so why do guys like* Dawn of the Dead *so much?* Again, the answer is simple: *Dawn of the Dead* is the ultimate male fantasy: an apocalyptic end-of-the-world scenario in which everything you ever wanted to own is relatively undamaged and up for grabs, with the only opposition being a bunch of slow moving, easily picked-off targets. That's why there's such a huge debate (trust me, ladies and guys who actually have a life, there really is a debate over this) re: slow zombies vs. fast zombies. Sure, fast zombies are scarier because they might actually catch you, but that's *exactly* why they completely undermine the fantasy. Nobody wants to be eaten by zombies during a zombie apocalypse; they just want to fortify the local sports stadium and then stockpile it with a bunch of cool stuff.

This book features short, no-nonsense (that means I use a lot of swear words) reviews of over 100 zombie movies you probably haven't seen (and okay, fine, a couple you probably have). These include current releases, obscure shorts, classic gut-munchers from the 1980's, and even a few moldy oldies from the days

2

when zombies were still hapless, pre-unionized saps working the sugarcane fields, and not ravenous, brain-eating nuisances. You'll notice I've also included several mummy movies in the mix, because let's face it, what is the mummy but a zombie, with less odious dietary habits, sporting a full body cast? (If you're wondering how someone sporting a full body cast can manage to run down and strangle so many people, you should keep in mind that most mummies are, in fact, dead, so being in a full body cast is the least of their problems. Seriously, you've got to stop over-thinking this shit.) Besides, I had no desire to have to compile all my mummy movie reviews into their own book later on. Seriously, who would even buy a book entirely about mummy movies? Fuck that jazz.

Aaah! Zombies!!

(2007)

Directed by Matthew Kohnen

Why are so many low-budget horror movies set, in whole or in part, in bowling alleys? Is there something inherently terrifying about bowling that I'm not aware of? Or do they all just think that they're the first one to come up with the "finding a head in the ball return" gag? Because trust me, you're not the first one to come up with that.

So in this cheapie, four surprisingly likeable young people (because most young people, ugh, right?) (except for young, easy chicks, of course) eat soft serve tainted with zombie toxin and become, you guessed it, zombies. The gimmick though is that they appear normal to each other, so they aren't even aware that they *are* zombies, which of course makes no real sense but at least this zombie movie *has* a gimmick, as opposed to being the 3000th remake of *Dawn of the Dead*, minus the cost-prohibitive shopping mall setting, of course. (Hey, if you and your film school dropout friends are working on remake #3001, I hear the bowling alley is available.) Of course *we* know they're zombies even if they don't, so there's none of that stuff rotund film legend Alfred Hitchcock Presents was famous for... Suspenders? Suspense, that's it. There's none of that, and the main characters' aggressive lack of self-awareness is a bit hard to swallow after a while, as are several other inexcusable lapses in logic, like the idea that the bowling alley would leave several untapped beer kegs outside for hours, where they could easily be stolen by the likes of me. There are a handful of passably humorous bits, I guess (Ha ha! Zombie in a sombrero! Okay, never mind.), but there's only so many "funny" scenarios a zombie can get itself into, no doubt explaining my failure in the 1990's to pitch my sitcom *Zombie Dad*, starring Fiona Apple as the hot, long-suffering daughter who repeatedly fucks the writer/producer in order to land the role. Er, forget you read that last part. Anyway, I've still got the script for the pilot on my hard drive if anyone's interested. I suppose it would be more appropriate to cast Fiona as the zombie now, but don't let that dissuade you. I'll still fuck her.

Abbott and Costello Meet the Mummy

(1955)

Directed by Charles Lamont

You know what Abbott and Costello really need to meet? Some fucking tits. Anyway, you know how these Abbott & Costello movies go: the fat one (does anyone really know which is which?) always finds a monster, or a dead body, or something, so he fetches the skinny one, but by the time they get back the body or whatever is gone, so the skinny one tells the fat one that he's an idiot and then slaps him across the face. It's classic. I guess. Unfortunately, this is not one of Abbott and Costello's better efforts, mainly because it raises too many questions that are never adequately answered. For example, how did the doctor studying the mummy in question not notice that it was fucking *alive?* And how did he turn on his tape recorder after *he* was dead? Why do all the Egyptian cops look like Klingons? Why doesn't anybody hook up the evil chick? She's fucking **hot**. And evil. Oh, and slightly deranged apparently:

HOT, EVIL CHICK: "My dear professor, some of the men I have met have acted like mummies, and others have certainly acted like they were 4000 years old. But I've never met one I was afraid of..."

Seriously, what in God's name is this broad talking about? I get the 4000-year-old part (that's why they invented Viagra), but how does a guy "act like a mummy"? Maybe it's some cosplay thing. At any rate, this movie is a complete disaster, and the titular (heh) mummy doesn't even get in on the action until the last twenty minutes, and even then one cat puts him out of commission (temporarily) just by hitting him over the head with a stick. The worst thing about this flick though is that, according to the credits, Abbott & Costello are supposed to be playing two guys named "Pete" and "Freddie", but the whole time they just call each other "Abbott" and "Costello"! Talk about lazy and unprofessional. As far as I'm concerned, next time Abbott & Costello should meet my foot. Right up their asses.

The Alien Dead

(1980)

Directed by Fred Olen Ray

This opens with an annoying redneck conversing in a ridiculously proper, *faux* intellectual manner, a trope/joke that was tiresome long before 1980 so needless to say I was pretty disappointed when this guy wasn't immediately ass-raped by zombies. They do get his no doubt long-suffering wife though, and, quickly dropping his absurd "smart" facade (trust me buddy, you weren't fooling anyone), he hightails it to the local sheriff, who just happens to be played by Buster Crabbe, best known for portraying both Flash Gordon *and* Buck Rogers in the 1930's. Not that anyone really cares how Buster Crabbe earned his spending money in his later years, but every review of *The Alien Dead* ever written feels compelled to point him out, like it's some appalling tragedy what he was reduced to, never mind that the people who write these reviews have likely never seen a 1930's Buster Crabbe movie and probably wouldn't watch one on a dare. Also, didn't Buster Crabbe ultimately die of tripping over a wastepaper basket? I mean really, how is that not more embarrassing than being in *The Alien Dead*, especially when this movie really isn't all that bad? Sure, it's kinda chintzy, and there's parts where it looks like they forgot to record any sound and then tried to obfuscate this with wildly inappropriate music, but it's full of pretty girls and (intentionally) ridiculous/hilarious dialogue, plus violence, gore, some tits, and it manages to exploit the whole 1970's/'80's comedic redneck craze (e.g. *Sheriff Lobo, The Dukes of Hazzard, Smokey and the Bandit, Deliverance*) without being anywhere near as aggressively repellant as, say *Redneck Zombies* (1987). Honestly, what's not to like? Don't be some crybaby Buster Crabbe apologist. He could've bagged groceries that summer if he'd really wanted to. Nobody put a gun to his head and forced him to take this gig.

All Souls Day: Dia de los Muertos

(2005)

Directed by Jeremy Kasten

This guy blows up a whole passel of Mexicans, who, fifty years later, return as Mexican zombies and wipe out the first luckless fucks who happen to turn up. Fifty more years pass, and now this cat and his girl are rolling into the very same town where all this shit went down, where they immediately ingratiate themselves with the locals by crashing right into some chick's funeral. And cue Dante Hicks from *Clerks* (1994) saying "Her fucking body fell out!" because that's exactly what happens. But dealing with this social faux pas, and the damage to their car, takes a back seat (heh) when it turns out that the girl in the coffin is still alive! They call the sheriff, who's so blatantly shady that you just know they're fucked, but, naturally, with their car out of commission they have no choice but to hang around and wait for the inevitable horror. Now, I don't know about you, but after all the horror movies I've seen, if my car ever breaks down in some weird-ass little burg and I see *anything* out of the ordinary – even something minor, like a housecat that knows how to flush the toilet (because, you know, he thinks he's people) – I am *walking* home. I don't care if it's a hundred miles back. You crazy yokel supernatural toilet-cat fucks aren't getting your hands on Mr. Satanism. Our main guy and girl aren't quite that motivated, but they do call some friends to come get them, and once our additional fodder shows up the undead beaners rise again and several people die. This flick is fairly gory and there are some tits, so overall it was pretty decent, although just once I'd like to see a zombie movie that doesn't include a "Let's barricade ourselves inside this building!" scene. I mean really, you can *run away* from zombies too, you know.

Ancient Evil: Scream of the Mummy

(1999)

Directed by David DeCoteau

I swear, the hack fucks who made this movie must've used some kind of complicated space-age math to determine exactly how little they could do and still technically end up with a mummy movie. Seriously, it's like mummy minimalism. Basically, an out-of-shape mummy ambles around somebody's house (oh, they claim it's some sort of research facility, but it's obviously just some Mexican doctor's summer home or something) until it's time for the big finale, in which a skinny, cross-eyed dork wearing a towel and a stripper cape tries to sacrifice an ugly virgin to Tic Toc the rain god and end the world. Honestly, this entire movie is a complete bag of shit: nothing happens, there's barely any blood, and the only passably cute chick is this blonde who's such a stupid fucking whore that it's almost not even worth seeing her tits, and she doesn't show them to us anyway. Also, if you're gonna sacrifice a virgin, isn't it standard operating procedure to tear her shirt off first? I know I said the virgin was ugly, but hell, the damn movie was almost over with zero prospects and that late in the game I'm willing to take just about anything. I guess you could say that this flick is the movie equivalent of a fat chick at last call, but that isn't entirely fair. This flick is more like getting dissed by the fat chick too and settling for eating out a homeless guy's asshole.

Babylon Fields

(2007)

Directed by Michael Cuesta

A TV series where the dead rise as zombies and then absolutely nothing happens? No, it's not Season 2 of *The Walking Dead*, it's *Babylon Fields*, the high-concept show where the zombies, instead of killing everyone, quietly re-assume their old lives and just hang around, rotting all over everything. I guess it's supposed to be all symbolic and shit, which might (understand I said *might*) work as a one-off movie, but as a regular TV series? Really, who wants to watch the adventures of characters like "Asshole Zombie Dad" when their own asshole dad is right there in the living room, guzzling beer and yelling at the Packers game? Still, I guess this setup *could* make for some interesting stories, although most of them would probably boil down to your standard, tired-ass "prejudice against some weird monster standing in for real-world prejudice" schtick. To be fair, there are hints that the zombies might start eating people eventually (once they're settled in, I guess), and one of the main characters is a highly sympathetic (read: hot) teenage redhead who's so fine that if this show *had* been picked up I probably *would* have tuned in every week, just to see what happened to her. Hopefully nudity.

It all would've been a lot more effective if the fucking zombies didn't *talk*. Hell, when two of them met in the cul-de-sac to bitch about their families and discuss their sex drives we'd practically drifted into sitcom territory, which once again brings us around to my proposed sitcom, *Zombie Dad*. Except in my show, of course, Zombie Dad actually eats people, forcing his daughter to go to zany lengths to keep the authorities from finding out. Every week some new, madcap adventure would result, but the daughter would always save the day in the end (learning a valuable lesson in the process, natch), and then she would have X-rated sex with her boyfriend, played by me. We'd have to cut out the sex scenes for network TV of course, but we'd film them every week anyway, sometimes three or four times, just to make sure we got them right. It's called professionalism, people.

Baron Blood

(1972)

Directed by Mario Bava

Long ago there was this evil baron who tortured and killed everyone and anyone he could get his hands on, and now his great-to-the-whatever-power grandson wants to use an incantation to bring him back to life. You know, just for kicks. The grandson figures it's no big deal, since he has a second incantation that will kill the baron again if he turns out to be too much of a douchebag: "If we don't dig him, we'll ditch him!" he explains to the hot chick who tags along. Too bad they end up losing the second spell when an inopportune gust of wind blows it into the fireplace. Really, you couldn't have weighed it down with your keys, or a pair of sunglasses or something? So the evil baron is on the loose, and the first thing he does now that he's risen from the dead is visit a doctor. Which, when you think about it, makes a lot of sense. I'm surprised more zombies don't do this. Of course the next thing on his to-do list is a killing spree, but his rampage isn't particularly impressive, the torture chamber that plays prominently into the story hardly gets a workout at all, and the main chick, who is truly smokin', never takes her clothes off. In short, like a hot chick who dies while still a virgin, this movie is a tragic waste of potential.

Black Demons

(1991)

Directed by Umberto Lenzi

Remember that episode of *The Cosby Show* where Theo visited the voodoo doctor? I was really hoping that one would play out a lot differently. The honky in this flick is interested in the voodoo too, but he gets more than he bargained for when some zombies pop out of the ground and start killing everybody. First they tear a hottie's eye out, then they do the same thing to an ugly chick, and finally they lay siege to the mansion everyone else is holed up in. The thrilling climax consists of a guy blowing zombies up with Molotov cocktails while the main chick's possessed brother chases her fat ass all over the house with an axe. There's not much gore, no tits to speak of, and there's too much fake, unbelievable shit, like some "wild" birds that are clearly chained down so they won't fly away, a spider on a string, and a chick who only owns two pairs of shoes. This all would've made for a relatively kickass episode of *Cosby* – especially if the zombies ate Rudy, because who didn't hate that reprehensible little cunt? – but as a legitimate zombie movie, it's a pretty sorry-ass example.

Incidentally, fuck you, Rudy. You knew better than to cut the pictures out of those expensive encyclopedias. Your "I'm just the baby" schtick might've fooled Bill Cosby, but it wouldn't fool me. If I'd been babysitting that day, I would have beaten your ass for so long you'd have earned a degree. And then I would've banged Vanessa.

Black Swarm

(2007)

Directed by David Winning

This single mom returns to her former hometown, even though it's such a hole that the mayor is reduced to roaming the streets, begging citizens not to relocate. Oh, and just to add injury to insult, there's a swarm of killer bees on the loose. These aren't just your run-of-the-mill killer bees though - these fuckers lay eggs in people and turn them into zombie slaves! I guess that makes them zom-bees. Ha! Brilliant. The story does take a few wrong turns – like the part where the daughter becomes queen of the bees (duh), or the when the mom, who I assumed was merely a disgusting whore, reveals her big secret, establishing herself as a lying, self-centered cunt too – but any flick based on the premise that zombies simply aren't enough, they have to be filled with killer bees too, is okay in my book. It's a shame our single mom ultimately survives the horror though; when that bitch told the main guy that leaving him at the altar, marrying his twin brother, and then lying to everyone about the paternity of their child was all **his** fault because "You should've fought harder to keep me," he should've knocked her goddamned teeth down her throat, and then shoved some of those killer bees right up her fucking ass.

Blood from the Mummy's Tomb

(1971)

Directed by Seth Holt

"I thought you'd never see it," says the main chick when her beau finally notices the ring her pop gave her. Frankly, I don't know how you could miss it - it's the cheapest, tackiest-looking thing I've ever seen that didn't wrap up the evening by blowing me. Apparently dad does all his gift shopping at that bank of bubblegum machines outside the grocery store.

Worse things are in store for this twat though, because it seems the ring originally belonged to this perfectly-preserved hottie dad unearthed in Egypt the very same day she was born. I so would've called dibs if I was at *that* tomb opening, and it looks like dad felt the same way, seeing as the catatonic hottie has spent the last 20+ years in his basement. "What are you doing down there, Dad?" "Nothing! Don't open the door!" The indisputable bad guy, meanwhile, actually wants to bring the hottie back to life. Why? There is some gibberish about her being "beyond good and evil", but I think it's mostly because she has big ol' titties. A few people do get killed along the way (most hilariously fake death: the joker who manages to crash his car into a tree even though the car is obviously standing perfectly still), but for the most part it's all pretty lame. Hell, even the catfight at the end is weak. Oh, and speaking of cats, there's one in this movie and according to the credits its real name is "Sunbronze Danny Boy". What kind of mick fag names their cat "Sunbronze Danny Boy"? Jesus.

Bog Creatures

(2003)

Directed by J. Christian Ingvordsen

Several evil Vikings, along with the chicks the violated (tough break, bitches) are killed and tossed into a bog, and when regular times roll around these college students unearth the lot of them and they revive as zombies. Now, the chick zombies are actually friendly (but not *too* friendly, which is fortunate because, you know, gross), but the Vikings just want to hack everyone to pieces with their trsuty swords, which means at this point you're sitting on a pretty solid premise for a movie: zombies with swords. They screwed the whole thing up though, and here's how:

First, there's the female professor who initially sends the college students into the bog. She's hot, but we never see her naked. That's strike one.

There are plenty of other cute chicks on hand, and none of them get naked either. Strike two.

The college students come across yet another cute chick, who's in shock. One of the girls finds a wet rag and cleans her up, while this pervo panty-sniffer watches through the window. This could have easily turned into a big naked rub-down/dyke scene, with some voyeurism thrown in for good measure. It doesn't though. Strike three.

There's a girl-on-girl knife fight at the end, but it's inexcusably lame and only lasts for a couple of seconds. Strike four.

And finally, we've got our Viking zombies, remember them? They do off some people, but the kills, instead of being gruesome, are totally weak. So that's strike five and while the wheelchair kid and your baby brother may get four strikes down at the ol' sandlot, you don't get five strikes even if you're a girl *and* just got out of the hospital. Suck my balls, *Bog Creatures*. You're riding the bench.

Buck Wild

(2013)

Directed by Tyler Glodt

"Damn coons," this old guy says when he hears something creeping around outside. I wonder if he means raccoons or... Anyway, I was hoping this flick was about has-been reality TV "star"/comediette Becky "Buckwild" Johnson, whom I desperately want to bone. (Those tits...) Unfortunately, it's just another "comedic" zombie movie, although it does kick off with an attack by a zombie dog, so that's something at least. Actually, as far as comedic zombie movies go this isn't too bad - it looks professional, the characters are likeable (the self-consciously crazy cousin could have been a super-annoying disaster in lesser hands, but here he's hilarious), there's some decent action, plenty of genuinely funny lines ("Anyone know a good attorney???"; "Is that a fish?"), and a pretty hot farmer's daughter type, although we never do see her tits so that is a mark against it. A couple of ideas really don't work (like the dumb zombie-as-therapist bit), and it ends with the oldest cliché in the zombie book (a siege on an isolated ranch house), but all told it's pretty damn good for a zom-com, and worth catching. Who says there's no more life in the zombie film? Ha ha! Get it? Hey, make your own jokes then. Fuck you. Unless you're Becky Buckwild, in which case please, please fuck me. Seriously, we'll make a pilot out of it. How does *Zombie Dad* sound to you?

The Cat Creature

(1973)

Directed by Curtis Harrington

This fool steals a mummy's amulet, so the mummy comes to life, transforms into a vampire cat, and starts knocking off random people who may or may not have, at one point in time or another, been in the general vicinity of said amulet. Usually the cat goes the direct route and leaps on the person's face, but in one case it hypnotizes this relatively passable piece (I wouldn't make a habit of it, but I'd definitely fuck her) and walks her right over her balcony. There was really no reason to kill this chick, by the way, unless vampire mummy cat was just punishing her for delivering this incomprehensible line after he turns down some milk:

PASSABLE PIECE: "Hey, don't tell me you're a champagne freak."

What? Also featured: the mom from *Family Ties*, who gets involved after taking a job at an occult bookstore. ("Once you learn the stock it'll be just like working in a delicatessen. Without having to smell the garlic," her boss explains. Again, what?) Also featuring one of the Felix Leiters (you know, from James Bond), a midget hooker, a detective test-driving his *film noir* quips ("Straight, huh? Why you could sleep on a corkscrew."), and an almost-makes-it-all-worth-it climax where the mummy, now back in traditional mummy form, throws down with a pack of stray cats. Overall though it's pretty boring, and I wouldn't recommend it unless you must see every brain-damaged cat-oriented horror movie out there, and if that's the case, might I also recommend *Sleepwalkers* (1992), *Strays* (1991), and possibly getting out of the house once in a while.

Children of the Living Dead

(2001)

Directed by Tor Ramsey

Okay, this starts off with a *Dawn of the Dead* style zombie outbreak, but then everybody forgets it ever happened and 14 years later we join some kids on their way to a concert. Except for the chick in the passenger seat (who's so goddamned hot that it's unfair to the rest of her gender, plus most gay guys) they're complete fucking write-offs, so it's only slightly tragic when a zombie steps in front of their van, panicking them into driving off a cliff. Later our undead jaywalker visits the cemetery where the kids have been buried and zombifies the lot of them, so I figured I knew where *this* story was going, but *Children of the Living Dead* is always one incomprehensible step ahead so suddenly it's *another* year later and **oh the humanity they're moving the headstones but not the bodies!** *You son of a bitch! You left the bodies and you only moved the headstones! You only moved the headstones!!! Why??? Why???*

For real, what the Christ-baiting fuck is going on? So far it's like three different zombie movies in one, all of which suck. And as if being completely nonsensical isn't bad enough, we also have to put up with stupid humor like this:

IDIOT: "I was wondering if you knew the name of a diner around here where I can get a decent breakfast?"

HEARING AID GUY: "You say you're looking for a miner with a black vest?"

The hilarity. And don't even get me started on the big redneck/zombie brawl at the end. What makes it all so sad is that there is some good stuff to be found here, if you're willing to look: the part where they find the guy who got buried alive works, the main zombie is pretty damn cool, there's the aforementioned hottie, and I definitely wouldn't mind sticking the brunette waitress who eventually becomes the main chick; she's looking mighty fine in those stylish black capris, and her rack alone could feed a whole family of zombies. Those minor assets aside though, this movie is a complete disaster. At the very least the waitress could've gotten naked.

Children Shouldn't Play with Dead Things

(1973)

Directed by Bob Clark

A party of actor-artist-hippie-faggots sporting the worst clothes in the entire fucking world piss off to this island where they cast a spell that's supposed to bring the dead back to life. Of course it doesn't work (because they're idiots; also, magic isn't real), so they content themselves with hauling a token corpse back to this nearby cottage where their leader – who's the biggest homo of all and says stupid shit like "The magnitude of your simplitude overwhelms me." – fucks around with it for a while and gives everybody else endless amounts of shit until even the dead are so goddamned sick of listening to him run his mouth that they actually DO rise so they can tear his ass to pieces and shut him the hell up. Ultimately the zombies attack the cottage and eat everybody, and then they steal the actors' boat and head for town, I guess to score some after-dinner drinks or something. Nothing happens until the last half hour of this movie, but the zombies look pretty boss when they finally show up, and the chicks are all definitely fuckable, which makes it extra tragic that not one of them ever gets naked. Seriously, aren't actor-hippie-artist type chicks generally total whores? What the hell's going on here?

Chiller

(1985)

Directed by Wes Craven

This dude has been cryogenically frozen (you know, like Walt Disney), I guess to be revived only when they discover the cure for truly awful hair. Ha ha! Seriously though, as the movie opens he's thawing out early due to technical incomptitude, so they decide they'd better fully revive him, and never mind the fact that if the cure for whatever condition he had when they froze him is now available (which it apparently is), they probably should have done this a long time ago. Multiple lawsuits are doubtlessly pending, but for the time being he heads home, where we learn that his dog hates him now, clearly identifying him as evil, because as we all know dogs instinctively hate evil people. And blacks. His dog hates him so much, in fact, that it hurdles a six-foot fence to get at him, like it's the goddamned bionic dog or something. He manages to kill it without too much effort though, so I doubt it'll be lending an assist to Jaime Sommers anytime soon. Maybe bionic Bigfoot would've had better luck.

Since our main guy is evil, and it's the 1980's, the next logical/most creatively barren move is for him is to become a Gordon Geico-style businessman, so that's exactly what happens. As the story plods along he makes an old man have a heart attack, spies on his step-sister while she's changing clothes, and beats the shit out of a chick at work, none of which so much as raises an eyebrow. But when he stops donating money to the church, the family pastor leaps into action, eventually convincing everyone that our main dude no longer has a soul. So his mom locks him in the freezer, at which point he turns into a zombie, giving her a pretty solid excuse to shoot him. This was made for 1980's television so of course it's entirely too tame, but I think "evil zombie businessman" is a pretty solid idea. I'm all for a sequel, where he returns from the grave again to fight Michael Moore.

(Note: Despite my little joke above, Walt Disney wasn't really cryogenically frozen, that's just an urban legend. Sources that claim otherwise are just confusing him with Hitler.)

Corpse Eaters

(1974)

Directed by Donald R. Passmore and Klaus Vetter

How can you possibly go wrong with a movie called "Corpse Eaters"? As a lark, four canucks (one of them actually says "eh?") cast a spell in a graveyard on Friday the 13th, inadvertently bringing the dead back to life as flesh-eating zombies. It's like a Canadian version of *Children Shouldn't Play with Dead Things*, except I think that movie was Canadian too. It's shorter though, and creepier, and considerably less obnoxious, and while the chicks aren't as hot at least one of them shows us her tits (in Canada, this is known as the "ugly chick's option"). The zombies look great, and when they chow down it's pretty graphic, but I did not appreciate the inclusion of that dumb gimmick where they show a visual "warning" before anything especially gruesome happens. In this case it's some middle-aged guy shoving a handkerchief into his mouth, like he's about to hurl, I guess. Are you kidding me? I'm watching a movie called fucking "Corpse Eaters". If I was worried about seeing a little gore I'd be, oh, I dunno, *doing pretty much anything else*. Seriously, I hate pussified shit like this. If you're gonna warn us every time there's repulsive horror, why not warn us when something sexy is about to happen too? Like maybe that middle-aged guy could be jerking off or something. He'd probably like it, too, the fucking pervert.

Corpses Are Forever

(2003)

Directed by Jose Prendes

Okay, I get that they're going for a James Bond thing here, but there has got to be a better zombie-oriented play on a James Bond title than "Corpses are Forever". How about "The Living Deadlights"? Yeah, that kinda sucks. "A View to a Corpse"? Nah. "You Only Live Twice" would work as-is, except they'd probably get sued... "Zombieraker"? "Corpsepussy"? (Ha ha! Gross.) "Never Say Dead Again"? Okay, fine, *Corpses Are Forever* it is. Unfortunately, it turns out this isn't really a super spy/zombie mash-up after all, it's more of an unmitigated disaster by way of something my girlfriend wouldn't even bother to swallow. The "story" involves one guy reliving the memories of another guy who's trying to find a serial killer who kidnapped his son while zombies are taking over the world because the Gates of Hell were opened by the serial killer who made a deal with the Devil that... I think you get the point. It's overly-ambitious without having any idea what it's doing, and as a result it's a convoluted disaster that doesn't know whether it's sucking or blowing. (Answer: both.) Instead of trying to make any sense out of this hopeless garbage I spent the running time laughing at the many punches that blatantly failed to connect, the main guy's Superman tattoo (what a tool), and all the over-the-hill scream queens who showed up for the party (know when to quit, hags). The only positive: one outstanding bikini babe, who gets maybe a ninety seconds of screen time. "Why don't I just shoot you and put you out of your misery?" says somebody at one point. I'd say that sums this movie up perfectly.

Cronos

(1993)

Directed by Guillermo del Toro

An antiquated junk dealer (By "antiquated" I mean the guy is old, not his junk. And by "junk" I mean rummage, not horse. By which I mean smack.) obtains a bizarre contraption that injects him with eternal life juice, the only downside being that, as we all know, eternal life always backfires in some horrific way. I mean look at Joan Rivers. This Howard Hughes-type who's been looking for the contraption soon gets wind and sends his weird-ass nephew around to acquire it, and when the decrepit old geezer won't play ball the nephew stuffs him into a car which he rolls over a cliff. Now, eternal life/irony were already taking their toll on the geezer (at one point, he was licking blood off the floor of a public bathroom), but after the cliff incident he's really messed up and more-or-less fully zombified. He does manage to find his way back to his little granddaughter though, one of those unnaturally quiet, shy movie children who never utters a single word. In short, she's unbelievably irritating, and I was praying that when gramps zombied out completely he would cave her goddamned head in or at the very least pull both her arms out of their sockets. I'll bet she'd make some noise then. Unfortunately that doesn't happen, and even when Zombie Granddad works over the bad guys the results aren't particularly gruesome. C'mon, old man, pull out their eyes, or eat their guts, or something. You're a fucking *zombie* fer chrissakes. Act like it.

Dance of the Dead

(2008)

Directed by Gregg Bishop

So it seems the local cemetery is of the *Dellamorte Dellamore* (1994) variety, complete with a caretaker who isn't too keen on letting the word get out. As pop culture references go that's not bad, but I much preferred the musical nod when the band auditioning to play prom goes with "Somebody's Gonna Get Their Head Kicked in Tonite", a super famous punk song actually written by and for Fleetwood Mac. (Don't tell any punks.) The typical high school lowjinks that make up the beginning of this movie are a bit too obvious and good-natured, kind of like a chick you dump after the second date, but once the zombies appear things pick up considerably: we've got zombies bursting out of their graves, several feet into the air, and then hitting the ground running; zombified dissection frogs; two zombies eating each other as foreplay; and it all builds up to a terrific, gory climax at the prom. "Why is this happening?" asks one chick. "End of the world," replies her friend. "God's flushing the toilet." Yeah, I've seen Sara Gilbert's *The Talk* too. I agree, whole-fucking-heartedly.

Dawn of the Mummy

(1981)

Directed by Frank Agrama

I know if you're a mummy your sack is probably all dried up and sealed in a jar someplace, but that doesn't mean you can't show some balls in the symbolic sense. That's what makes this movie so awesome - instead of engaging in your typical low-key mummy activities (shuffling, half-heartedly choking people out, crying over some ex-girlfriend he broke up with *years* ago) this mummy is all about kicking ass and taking names, and he's all out of names. It starts when some tomb raiders invade his eternal pad. They're in the process of looting the place when – wouldn't you know it – some models working on an "account" for a "top fashion magazine" (yeah, that doesn't sound completely bogus; I see a lot of hard lessons, learned the hard way, in *their* futures) show up and decide to use the tomb for a photo shoot. Now, any criminals worth their salt would just engage in a quick and dirty mass murder – possibly garnished with some rape – and then head for the hills with the swag. Not these dipshits though; they actually humor the models and it's all in serious danger of deteriorating into a zany farce when, just in the nick of time, the mummy and his zombie army make the scene and start killing everybody. It's pretty damned gory too, with eyes gouged out, faces melting off, people eaten alive, and intestines flying every which way, including loose. I wasn't too impressed with the chicks they scrounged up to play the models (I wouldn't be interested in most of these second-tier also-rans if they were modeling my cock in their mouth), but sometimes repulsive horror is enough and this is definitely one of those times. *Dawn of the Mummy* rocks.

Day of the Dead 2: Contagium

(2005)

Directed by Ana Clavell and James Glenn Dudelson

Jesus fucking Christ do I hate the movie *Day of the Dead*, and yes, I am referring to the original *Day of the Dead*, not the remake, although that one sucks too and we'll get to it in a moment. The first two zombie flicks the *Day of the Dead* guy made – *Night of the Living Dead* (1968) and *Dawn of the Dead* (1978) – were awesome, but *Day of the Dead* is just a bunch of annoying, obnoxious fuckstains yelling stupid, boring shit at each other, until they're finally eaten by zombies, and not a moment too soon but at least an hour too late. *Day of the Dead* sucks so much ass that when it first came out back in 1985 they actually had to truck extra ass in to the theaters for it to suck on. What really pisses me off though is the army of pinheads who wanted *Day of the Dead* to be good so badly that – after bitching about it for a while – they retroactively decided that it *was* good, evidence to the contrary be damned. People who champion *Day of the Dead* are like the people who back a really crummy sports team and then lose their shit when they go 2-10 every year. It doesn't matter how bad you want it, assholes: *Day of the Dead* will always be a miserable piece of shit.

So that brings us to Part 2. In this one, several loonies and tards are turned into zombies, which would be fine except for the fact that *they all have psychic links with each other*, and if there's one thing I hate more than girls who won't swallow it's motherfucking psychic links. *Why do movies and books, even ones that aren't specifically about psychic links, always insist that a huge percentage of the population has a psychic link?* There you are watching a perfectly good movie and suddenly, out of the blue, there's some asshole with a psychic link. It pisses me off. Fortunately, this movie was already pretty dumb, so it's not like the psychic links make it all that much worse. I mean, a virus that manifests itself as a swarm of little Tinker Bell fairies? Zombies cracking wise? And what the fuck is with the hottie who goes from zero to nine months pregnant in approximately 24 hours? Don't ask me, because *the movie never bothers to explain this.* Maybe Jesus was in there. This flick is reasonably gory once the zombies get down to business, but that doesn't actually happen until over an hour in so it's hardly worth the trouble.

An absolute pile, in the grand *Day of the Dead* tradition. I swear, if they make a Part 3 somebody's gonna end up in a sack by the side of the road.

Day of the Dead

(2008)

Directed by Steve Miner

If you ask me. *Day of the Dead* (1985) is exactly the type of horror movie they *should* be remaking, unlike all these pointless remakes of perfectly serviceable flicks like *A Nightmare on Elm Street* (1984/2010), *My Bloody Valentine* (1981/2009), or a version of *The Toolbox Murders* (1978) where Juliet Landau doesn't even get naked (2004). After all, the original *Day of the Dead* was immediately recognized as a game-changing (or at least diaper-changing) steamer when first released, and it remains a steamer no matter how many simpering, delusional fucktards retroactively insist that it's a masterpiece. Seriously, if you think the original 1985 *Day of the Dead* is a masterpiece, then you probably think the poop you've been flinging at your living room wall is *Whistler's Mother*, or that Seth MacFarlane actually passed Comp II without blowing anyone.

So here's the remake and, good news first, there is some entertaining chaos early on (I especially liked the part where a chick was eaten by zombies who were on fire. The meal was raw, but the diners were well done!), but not only are the zombies the fast kind (which automatically sucks) but sometimes they're artificially sped up too, so that any second you expect them to drop whatever they're doing so they can chase Benny

Hill. And since when do zombies jump around like Batroc the Leaper? (What? Oh, look it up.) Some of them even crawl across walls and ceilings; apparently in this universe, when you die, you receive some of Spider-Man's abilities. (I wonder if that includes the ability to boff Kirsten Dunst? It should.) There's too many shitty, computer-generated cartoon effects, they kill off the best character (the fat D.J.) way too soon, and I got really, really tired of hearing people dismiss/explain shit away by saying "It's complicated." Yeah, dialogue and motivation *are* complicated, but at least make the effort, you lazy fucking hacks. By the end we've got zombies dropping out of the ceiling to grab people and the whole thing has obviously deteriorated into just another dumb, generic monster movie. Still, "dumb and generic" trumps "mind-rapingly awful" every day of the week and twice on federal holidays, so I'm still declaring this version marginally better than the original, like, say, the difference between stepping in shit barefoot, or with your shoes on. It still sucks, but at least there's more to it than a bunch of unlikeable assholes screaming "fuck" at each other for 100 minutes.

Dead & Buried

(1981)

Directed by Gary Sherman

So the sheriff who's on the case is driving along when he accidentally runs into a pedestrian, somehow tearing the poor bastard's arm completely off. But then, amazingly, the guy gets up, retrieves his arm, and just runs away! It's a wild scene full of unanswered questions, and if they had opened with it they really might've been onto something here. Instead, this occurs 45 minutes in, long after we're already bored shitless with this clunky, badly-written, go-nowhere movie. The plot concerns some small town yokels who are on a killing spree, offing various strangers in wildly (and generally unnecessarily) convoluted ways, and taking plenty of photographs of each and every murder in the process, with plans, no doubt, to post them on Facebook later. Stupid assholes. Truth be told, with the exception of the brunette hitchhiker, who's pretty tasty, the morons they ice aren't likely to be missed, but this hardly matters since the dead people all pop right back to life, after which they immediately settle in and insist that they've always been locals and what the hell are you talking about, boy? Since there's a good chance you caught the title of this book before you read this far, or picked up at least some clues along the way, you've probably guessed that they're zombies now, but when the guy responsible finally reveals himself (does being the most obvious suspect even warrant a spoiler warning?) he refuses to explain how he did it, and just barely touches on why (if I recall correctly, it was some variation on "Because"). The story makes almost no sense, the acting is hammier than Christmas dinner, and there's endless stretches where nothing of consequence happens at all, which I'm guessing is this movie's definition of "suspense". Somehow this turd has acquired a bit of a reputation, but so did the girl at my high school who supposedly had three abortions so don't be fooled. If you wanna see a creepy "small town zombies" flick that actually delivers, check out *Messiah of Evil* (1973) instead, which is hardly a perfect movie but compared to this disaster, yes, it is.

Dead and Deader

(2006)

Directed by Patrick Dinhut

Really? Your title is an ungrammatical play on *Dumb & Dumber* (1994)? This movie isn't even a comedy! Scorpions are crawling inside people and turning them into zombies (okay, maybe it is a comedy), and one unlucky fucker suffering this absurd fate is Clark "Lois & Clark" Kent. I guess he's still got a little Superman in him though, because he ends up becoming a good zombie (gay), rounds up entirely too many sidekicks, and leads them into battle against the evil zombies. This flick has the worst annoying black sidekick coming back to life cop-out since *Jaws 4*, and the good guys could've saved the day a lot sooner if they didn't stop every two minutes to make some lame reference to another movie. (I swear to God, if I hear one more person bring up *Star Wars* in a flick that isn't actually about *Star Wars* I'm gonna start kicking people in the nuts. And rest assured, you're at the top of that fucking list, Kevin Smith. I know that if you remove "Star Wars references" from of your bag of tricks that doesn't leave much besides "farting", but that's your problem, fat man.) Those debits aside, there is a ton of gore, one pair of tits, and a zombie midget, so amazingly enough this actually ends up being an okay movie. I was a little put off by the big speech Zombie Clark gives at the end though, where he says he's gonna become one of those guys who roams the country doing odd jobs and conveniently turning into a monster just in time to save the day, à la David "The Hulk" Banner or Eric "Werewolf" Cord. This strongly implies that someone actually thought this premise might make a good TV series, which I suppose wouldn't be the height of idiocy but it would definitely be renting space in the same building. Naturally, I have a better idea: drop the secondary characters, bring on Teri Hatcher, and revamp it as *Zombie Lois & Clark*. And think of all the money you'd save on zombie makeup, because Teri Hatcher sure wouldn't need any. Seriously, have you seen that bitch lately? She looks like she got her face done at Mummies R Us for half price, and then used the bread she saved to buy new tits at the Used-Up Single Mom Superstore. It's hard to believe something so fine could go so downhill so fast, but it just goes to show why you should never pursue a woman based based solely on her looks. At the very least she should be rich too.

The Dead Next Door

(1989)

Directed by J.R. Bookwalter

"*The Jeffersons* and *Sanford and Son* will not be shown at their regularly scheduled time this evening..." the Emergency Broadcast Systems informs us as the zombie apocalypse begins (in Akron, Ohio, and no surprise there since they had such a huge head start). That made me laugh. But after this we jump ahead a few years and focus on an ~~elite~~ "Zombie Squad" that apparently travels far and wide to terminate some zombies, but drives right past others en route without taking so much as a pot shot at them. Okay, really, if your job is to eliminate the infectious zombie scourge, I think you need to make it a point to eliminate *every* zombie you see, not be all selective because you haven't had your coffee yet, or because the zombie in question owed you money when it was alive and you're still secretly hoping for a cure so you can get your fifty bucks back. And speaking of a cure, it seems there *is* one, maybe, so our lead Zombie Squad is off to Akron, accompanied by a scientist wearing a novelty baseball cap, to find it. Unfortunately, once there they run afoul of a religious cult run by a Jim Jones type (named "Reverend Jones" - so inventive!), who wants the zombie apocalypse to continue because it's God's will, or confirms the Rapture, or some such shit. Which does sounds like something a churchy type might do. There is plenty of over-the-top gore, and I wouldn't mind humping the blonde (understand that I wouldn't drive to Akron for it – or for anything else, for that matter – but if she was on hand and begging for it, I wouldn't *mind*), but the characters are all complete fucking morons ("I'll just put my fingers/hand/ whatever right in this zombie's mouth..."), it's laughably short (and still features *eight* goddamned minutes of end credits - padding much?), and the main guy sounds *exactly* like Bruce Campbell which isn't necessarily a bad thing, but it is weird and kind of distracting. *The Dead Next Door* tries to do the zombie apocalypse on a budget of nothing so it definitely gets points for being ambitious, but so does the chick who gave me a handjob when she interviewed to be my new PA, and I didn't end up liking her either.

Dead Season

(2012)

Directed by Adam Deyoe

Dead Season? Like the season of *Buffy the Vampire Slayer* where they introduced Dawn Summers? Ha ha! Don't get me wrong, I wouldn't even give Sarah Michelle directions to the bathroom if Michelle Trachtenberg was at the party, but that "Key" shit was fucking *weak*.

Anyway, most Americans haven't even planned for their retirement, but everyone's got a plan for the zombie apocalypse, and this plan almost always involves sailing to some apocryphal uninhabited island, where they'll live out their days drinking beer from hemisected coconuts and fucking the sixteen Catholic schoolgirls they rescued along the way. The main crew in this movie has the same idea, minus the schoolgirls, but early on it's obvious that they haven't really thought it through, since they forget to check their boat for zombies before they cast off *and* run out of gas along the way. Somehow two of them do manage to reach their destination though: DeSoto Island, which, according to their map, is a land mass roughly the size of Rhode Island, located not too far off the Florida coast. Of course if this place actually existed it would be a major population center and tourist destination, but this movie is stupid so it's almost entirely deserted. There is a dedicated zombie survivalist group holed up there though, but our heroes quickly take issue with this group's more extreme policies (namely the murder/cannibalism) so before long discord is sown and you can probably guess the rest. This flick features your typical zombie gore, some mediocre tits, and throwaway lines that take pains to tie it into both the original *Night of the Living Dead* and *28 Days Later* (2002), which, frankly, I found entirely too precious. In short, it's pretty fucking average, and considering the glut of zombie movies out there, "average" just ain't cutting it. My advice? Take a *Season* pass. Ha ha! "Season pass." I don't know how I come up with this stuff.

Dead Set

(2008)

Directed by Yann Demange

Before it even begins, this zombie/reality series mash-up is at a serious disadvantage, because it's intimately tied in to *Big Brother*, a program I can't even be bothered to acknowledge the existence of much less watch. You'll notice I said that the series was at a disadvantage, not me, and this is 100% accurate because it's TV's job to entertain me, and if I'm missing out on some important information I need for that to happen then it's the show's responsibility to fill me in, not my responsibility to try to figure it out. And, as much as I do not want to get caught up in this debate, I am getting pretty tired of "fast" zombies. The ones that just sort of putter around are, I dunno, creepier somehow. I guess it is more intense if they can actually chase you down, but that hardly matters in this case because all the action scenes in *Dead Set* look like they were shot by an unbalanced washing machine. Christ damn it, I am so sick of this fucking bullshit. When did "not being any good at your job" become the primary requisite for being a professional cameraman? You know what would be considerably more rewarding than watching *Dead Set*? Beating the guy who shot it until he had nerve damage, and then watching *him* shake around for three hours.

Don't think I'm gonna stop bitching just because I started a new paragraph. Another problem with *Dead Set* is that it's almost entirely about people who suck. Even the characters who aren't reality show types are unbelievably annoying. The worst has to be the twat with the gun: the second she starts cunting off you realize that, once again, someone has confused "tough, independent woman" with "obnoxious fucking bitch". And what is with the producer dude? He ends up trapped in a room with a perfectly doable bim and all he does is insult her! Look, Oswald, it's the end of the fucking world. I don't care if you're stuck in there with Snooki; under those circumstances you shut your damn pie hole and tap that shit.

So, to summarize, here's what's wrong with this miniseries:

1. It's a dumb idea based on a stupid reality show that no one except lame fags cares about
2. The zombies are the less creepy, trying-out-for-the-track-team kind
3. You can't see what's going on due to hack-wit camerawork by assholes
4. Nearly every character is a douchebag
5. The title is a pun, and that's almost never acceptable

Oh, and this isn't technically a slam, but I did find it extremely disturbing when, long after the zombie shit has hit the global fan, one cat turns on a television and *Big Brother* is still on the air. Apparently, even after the zombie apocalypse, there will still be reality shows. Like cockroaches and Donald Trump, man.

Dead Snow

(2009)

Directed by Tommy Wirkola

Subtitles? Are you fucking kidding me? Reading a Nazi zombie movie is like hiring a full orchestra to back Andrew W.K. And what the fuck does "Dead Snow" even mean, anyway? Is it some foreign idiom, like "the dead pants"? Or did they just figure zombies... snow... fuck it, "Dead Snow"? Christ, at least call it "Dead Cold" or something. Try to make a little goddamned sense. And while we're on this subject, *Dead Snow*, don't go to great lengths to establish that there's no cell phone service where your movie is taking place, and then have someone make a cell phone call just to set up one cheap gag. We don't have super-Alzheimer's, you condescending fucking movie. We remember shit that happened less than an hour ago.

The story: some losers and their sub-par girlfriends are chilling at a friend's cabin, being utterly lame, when this old guy shows up, acts like a raging dick for a while, and then tells them an absurd story about Nazi zombies which, tough break for them, turns out to be true. Of course the zombies kill our Crazy Old Guy Who Warned Everybody first, just like they do in every movie where he appears, which always leads me to wonder why he suddenly decided to break his silence in the first place. I mean, he's obviously made it to a ripe old age via a well-thought-out, two-pronged approach – healthy living and not warning anyone about the Nazi zombies – so what made him change his routine this time? And what's the deal with Nazi zombies anyway? If one of them bites you, do you automatically become a Nazi as well as a zombie? If not, how do you justify hanging out, exclusively, with Nazi zombies? I mean, you can't be all "Yeah, I like the eating human flesh aspect, and the music, but I just don't buy into their political ideology," because that would be the height of hypocrisy. But at the same time, being a zombie, who else is gonna take you in? It's a quandary, and I don't envy any politically on-the-fence Nazi zombies, I'll tell you that.

Death Valley: The Revenge of Bloody Bill

(2004)

Directed by Byron Werner

In a scene that's undeniably awesome, a drug dealer stumbles into this desert ghost town where zombies come swarming out of *everywhere* to take him down. Later another drug dealer shows up looking for the first one, hijacking several kids (and their coach) in the process and forcing them to drive him into the desert to find the guy. Okay, seriously, was kidnapping all these people really necessary? I mean, wouldn't it have been easier to just rent a car from Avis or something? Maybe he has bad credit. Anyway, they all end up stranded in the same zombie-infested ghost town, and that's when the zombies start peeling faces off, impaling people with swords, and, of course, eating everybody. And while our drug dealer may not pay his bills promptly (bad credit, remember?) he does pack plenty of heat, which comes in handy when he decides to go out in a true blaze of glory, pulling a full-on coke-fueled Scarface on a whole mess of zombies. Eventually the only human left standing is the hot redhead, but, lucky break for her, she looks exactly like the head zombie's dead sister so she manages to get close enough to decapitate the fucker. A hugely entertaining zombie movie. The only misstep: they never show the redhead naked! It's a shame, because she sure does look tasty. Especially when she's covered with blood.

Decay

(2012)

Directed by Luke Thompson

Remember back in 2008, when everyone was convinced that revving up that Large Hadron Collider over in Switzerland was going to destroy the world? (Spoiler warning: it didn't.) Well, in no way adding to these fears, some employees at the CERN facility where the LHC is located actually ran with the idea and shot a zombie movie there. In it, some internecine sabotage results in zombies, who spend the rest of the movie chasing our main characters around the place. The gore is merely adequate (some head shots, a fist through a torso, one dismembered date), and, location aside, the particulars are nothing new, but what makes this movie thoroughly watchable is main chick Zoë Hatherell, who is so eminently delectable that she could sell her used panties as coffee filters. And, as crazy as it sounds in a potential scream queen, apparently she's an honest-to-fuck physicist too! Just one more victory for science. There's a nice little twist at the end, Zoë Hatherell has a nice little rear end, we get to see parts of the CERN facility that only employees and terrorist supervillains usually see, we get to see Zoë Hatherell in a short skirt, the movie looks pretty good from a technical standpoint, and Zoë Hatherell looks pretty good from an everything standpoint. In the end it appears that

CERN has kicked off a full-on zombie apocalypse, so as public relations this is definitely an F, but as entertainment, I give it a solid C.

Deliver Me to Hell

(2010)

Directed by Logan McMillan

This was produced by Hell Pizza of New Zealand to promote their free-pizza-for-a-year contest, but it's easily better than half the movies in this book and pretty much solidifies Hell Pizza as the coolest goddamned pizza joint on the planet. It's an interactive video where you get to choose what the main guy does at certain points; there's only five choices, but one always gets him killed, sometimes spectacularly, so it's worth checking out all the permutations as you play through. His/your mission? Simple: zombie apocalypse be damned, a particularly fuckable hottie has ordered a pizza, for delivery, and you have to get it to her. It looks like they spent a bundle making this, it's just as violent and gory as you'd expect a zombie movie to be, and, best of all, *it's legitimately funny*. In fact, it kind of reminded me of the classic short story "Beer Run", from the old John Skipp/Craig Spector zombie anthology *Still Dead: Book of the Dead 2*. In that one, these folks who have successfully fortified themselves against the zombie apocalypse are forced to periodically brave the undead hordes anyway, because they keep running out of beer. "Beer Run" is, by far, the best story in that collection and, if I recall correctly, one of the few in which someone's dick isn't eaten. I'll tell ya, that book sure was obsessed with eating dick.

Diary of the Dead

(2007)

Directed by George A. Romero

I can't even begin to tell you how tired I am of these fucking *Night of the Living Dead* sequels. There hasn't been a good one since Part 2 in 1978, but the dude behind them just keeps churning the damn things out, like someone who eats too much Mexican food and can't stop shitting. This one goes it one worse by being the hand-held *Blair Witch* take, and it's so goddamned annoying that I couldn't even get through it the first time. Instead, I turned it off about fifteen minutes in and got drunk until I puked. On purpose. It was time better spent, believe me. Not making it all the way through a movie always makes me feel like a quitter though; I mean, I've survived *Frozen Flesh* (2008), *The Studly Coalition* (2006), *The Christmas Wife* (1988), even *Van* fucking *Helsing* (2004), and I'll be damned if I let this dung heap defeat me. So here we are, and from the dumb beginning where people are (ugh) making a movie and dropping trite observations ("Can somebody please explain to me why girls in scary movies always have to like fall down and lose their shoes and shit?"), to the slapdash story that feels like it was written by someone having a brain hemorrhage, to the awful cartoon effects they felt the need to slip in, to the endless contrived convolutions they jump through to constantly have people filming this shit when they should be running for their life (or trying to save someone else's), right up to the very end with its false sense of weary outrage, every second of this movie belongs in a primer on how to irritate the audience. It's like Phil Spector's "Wall of Sound", except in this case it's a Wall of Suck. And it's not like there's anything new here; except for the zombie who gets beaned in the head with a jar of acid and the zombies in the swimming pool we've seen all these bits in previous *...of the Dead* movies. It's just the same tired old shit, once again spewing out of this guy's one-note rectum. He should've called it "Diarrhea of the Dead".

Dorm of the Dead

(2006)

Directed by Donald Farmer

If two blonde hotties were clearly zombies, but were still pretty fresh, would you go for the threesome? Yeah, me too. The guy at the beginning of this movie sure ends up regretting it though. Meanwhile, some lesbianism is going on (damn, so far this movie is awesome), but that's soon interrupted by one lesbian's boyfriend (once again, someone is completely unclear on the concept), who loses his shit when he catches them (must be a glass-is-half-full kinda guy) and probably would have killed her if the walking dead didn't get him first. So why all the zombies? You won't believe this: the zombie outbreak was intentionally started by the main chicks' professor, solely to keep his wife from finding out that he was boffing a student. That's right, instead of just sending his little side dish on her way with an easy A or (the smart play, since she's cute) simply continuing to fuck her, *he turned her into a highly-infectious, flesh-eating zombie.* Most of the chicks are well-cast (read: hot) and there are some bodacious tits on display, but once you're over that (it took me about 40 minutes) this movie borders on life-changingly awful. The plot is utterly retarded, it looks like shit, the sole joke that works ("Let's all go to the lobby...") is dragged out for so long that it stops working, and it features some of the worst acting imaginable, aggravated by the fact that people who are supposedly interacting often aren't even in the same room at the same time. Honestly, was it really that difficult for every actor in a particular scene to request the same shift off at Burger King? *Dorm of the Dead* (2006) is moronic, it's tone deaf, and, worst of all, it's an inexcusable waste of some pretty admirable on-screen talent. By which I mean tits, obviously.

Evil Grave: Curse of the Maya

(2004)

Directed by David Heavener

This ugly skank and her disgusting slob of a fiancé move into a house that's haunted by wetback zombies. First on the zombies' to-kill list: two crooks who've been smuggling Mexicans into the country, Mexicans that are worth, according to one of them, "four thousand bucks". Wow. That's a lot of lawns. Next the zombies waste the slob and come after the skank, but this smarmy creep she fucked previously shows up and saves her, after which they send the zombies to Mayan zombie heaven via some idiotic, Children of the Corn-tinged horseshit. It's not over yet though, because a zombie baby got a piece of the smarmy guy along the way, so now *he* turns into a zombie, only to be shot (by a retard) and then hit by lightning (I assume by God, who, by this point, is probably as fed up with this crap as I am). Then, just to make this movie completely incomprehensible, the skank adopts a little zombie girl from Central America and it eats a Chinese midget.

Seriously, what the fuck?

Evil Unleashed: The Mummy

(2003)

Directed by Joe Castro

This insanely hot Egyptian piece kills herself so she'll live forever, which seems counter-intuitive but she really is beyond fine so I'm just going to assume she knows what she's doing. She's subsequently mummified ("You wrap that up and save it for later!" -My mom), and thousands of years later these cats dig her up only to be immediately killed, in a bit that may well re-define comedy, by a bunch of flying, plastic scorpions. Later someone with more money for shipping & handling than sense has the mummy delivered to the worst community college ever (seriously, they have finals on the *weekend*), where this professor brings her back to life so she can go on a rampage. A generous portion of this rampage consists of dancing around like a Fourth Dynasty slut and showing off her amazing rack though, so screw all these drive-thru college fucks, I'm rooting for the mummy. After she rips a few more hearts out (she stole mine the first time she took off her top) an ugly blonde and a sub-mediocre redhead try to destroy her, but seriously, a mummy-babe of this caliber does not deserve to lose out to a couple of also-ran bitches who couldn't even screw their way into a real college. And apparently *Evil Unleashed* agrees with me, because I'm happy to report that, in the end, the mummy wins.

Face of the Screaming Werewolf

(1964)

Directed by Jerry Warren

Why is it that the movies with the most lurid titles are always the lamest of them all? Two mummies are discovered in a pyramid in the Yucatan: a classic mummy, like the one you probably envision starring in old Hollywood flicks, and an Aztec mummy, the non-union Mexican equivalent best known for once fighting a robot called, well, "The Robot". Now, the Aztec mummy is actually alive when they find it and has to be subdued, but later these mad scientists steal the classic mummy and try to revive *it* using all this wild machinery, only later realizing that if they just steal the Aztec mummy, which is already alive, they'll be eliminating a difficult, costly step. Here's the twist that justifies the title though: the classic mummy also happens to be a werewolf! Eventually he wakes up, wolfs out, and offs one of the scientists, but he doesn't get far after that, immediately collapsing with what appears to be a throat problem. Maybe he needs a Halls. The Aztec mummy does manage to get away though, only to be hit by a car and, well, that's the end of him. Okay, seriously, the monsters aren't even going to fight? What the fuck? The werewolf finally escapes while the scientist in charge of watching him is out buying groceries, and, following his natural lupine instincts, he grabs a random chick, carries her up the side of a building à la King Kong, then brings her right back down via the stairs and leaves her on the sidewalk! (As a workout you can't beat it, but as the opening salvo to a rampage, it's pretty unimpressive.) In a possible bid to redeem himself the werewolf quickly grabs a second broad and takes her back to the lab, but by now these detectives who are theoretically on the case have finally zeroed in on him, and they... get an early start on the paperwork, because the werewolf has already been killed by one of the mad scientists.

And so the movie ends twice as pointlessly as it began, with all of us the losers.

The Fallen Ones

(2005)

Directed by Kevin VanHook

It can't be easy to make a mummy movie that's even stupider than *The Mummy Returns* (2001), but these guys took on the challenge and God damn 'em, they actually succeeded. Our key players are, in no particular order:

- A fallen angel
- A hot blonde, who's foisted on us as an intelligent, capable woman but is so dumb that every time someone uses a word bigger than "Fuck me" she's completely baffled and they have to explain it to her
- A giant mummy
- An evil cult

Okay, so the fallen angel wants to screw the dumb blonde and end the world, I guess in that order, and for some reason that I can't be bothered to remember this necessitates bringing the giant mummy back to life. Following the logic here, you'd expect a long-form giant mummy rampage to occur next, but as ridiculous as that would be it wasn't quite ridiculous enough for the fuckshit morons who made this piece of crap. Instead, everyone is suddenly attacked by a huge, wooden robot, operated by the evil cult using a primitive rope-and-pulley system. It looks like a Shogun Warrior built by Webelos. Oh, and did I mention that *at no point before it appeared did anyone mention this robot or so much as hint that it even existed?* That's right, it might as well have climbed, fully-formed, out of someone's ass, although now that it's here it might be kinda cool if the good guys commandeered it and used it to fight the giant mummy, right? Ha ha! Your puny human logic can suck *The Fallen Ones'* dick. Instead, the good guys tip the robot into a hole and completely forget about it, preferring to deal with the giant mummy the old-fashioned way: by screaming while it eats them. I kid, I kid. Actually, they blow up a dam and the mummy is destroyed in the ensuing flood. Because that's so much more satisfying than "giant mummy and wooden robot fight". Honestly, I don't know who had final approval over these Sci-Fi Channel movies back in 2005, but I'll tell you this: if some clowns came into *my* office proposing a movie that featured a giant wooden robot and a giant mummy and *the robot and the mummy didn't fight*, they would never work in this fucking town again. That bullshit may have passed muster back in the *Screaming Werewolf* era, but this is the 21st century and nowadays our monsters fight each other, dammit. That, or they molest a few teenage girls. I'm good either way.

Fear of the Living Dead

(2010)

Directed by Randy Smith

We open on a hottie, and before you know it, she's axin' a zombie. With an actual axe, I mean, she's not *axin'* him a question. She's not a spokesperson for 1-800-ASK-GARY. Several more zombies taste our hottie's wrath, and I was completely in love by the time she crossed paths with another human being. And wouldn't you know it, it's a fucking dude, who, being quite possibly the last man on Earth following a worldwide zombie apocalypse, will almost certainly tap that primo ass. Some guys have all the luck. Astoundingly enough, that's not what happens though. Instead, it turns out that this dude is part of a group seeking a cure for zombie apocalypses, so when he learns that the chick may be immune to zombie bites he confirms this with a blood sample and then immediately shoots her in the head and puts her body on ice. "This girl's got the most important blood in the world," he tells his two cohorts. Is that a fact? *Then why would you **kill** her and prevent her body from producing any more of it???* From a technical standpoint this movie looks pretty damn good, and the main chick looks even better (especially her ass), but there's just no getting past the fact that the entire premise is retarded as shit. You stupid fucking assholes; next time learn some basic biology before you try to make a zombie movie.

FleshEater: Revenge of the Living Dead

(1988)

Directed by S. William Hinzman

This joker pulls a stump out of the ground, and underneath there's a zombie! The zombie makes short work of him, then it impales another guy with a pitchfork and rips his fat pig of a date's stomach open and pulls out... her heart? I knew it! I *knew* fat people's hearts were located in their stomachs! Fuck you, Wikipedia, I am vindicated. Pretty soon there's zombies everywhere, and they roam around killing randoms for a while until somebody finally rounds up a bunch of hayseeds to hunt down their undead asses. Remember that part in *Dawn of the Dead* where all the rednecks were just hanging out, drinking Iron City beer, and casually shooting zombies? The end of this movie is essentially a longer version of that. The best bits are when two kids have such a long conversation about how in love they are that you know they're going to die, and when a barn is burned down for absolutely no reason. "I don't want anything coming out of that barn - alive *or* dead!" says the sheriff. What? You know the people who made this movie only torched that barn because someone told them they could. All told, it's a pretty impressive zombie flick: there's plenty of blood & gore, lots of tits (too bad that, except for one fairly tasty cheerleader, the chicks are pretty rogue), and best of all you can make a drinking game out of it: just chug every time they show someone wearing a jean jacket. A great party movie.

Flight of the Living Dead: Outbreak on a Plane

(2007)

Directed by Scott Thomas

You know, I'm really only seeing two ways that this can play out: the zombies are at one end of the plane, and chase everyone to the other end or the zombies are in the middle of the plane, and chase people in both directions. Either way, I can't see this flick lasting more than twenty minutes, tops, and that includes sufficient "character development" and a part where one of the stewardesses joins the mile-high club via her butt. And does there *always* have to be a prisoner on the flight who's being transferred somewhere by the cops? AND a nun? Hey, where's the little girl who needs a heart transplant? They could've revealed that the donor heart was on board too, and then had an ironic scene where the zombies ate it.

Of course nothing anywhere near as distasteful and awesome as that happens, and this movie takes forever to get down to business (the beginning, where we meet all the unlikable dickweeds who are gonna die before we remember who they were anyway, is boring as piss), but once the zombies get their groove on they fuck some people *up* and there's plenty of action and gore to go around. I get the feeling this one would've been way cooler if someone had thought to make it in 1980, but aside from a few unbelievably fake cartoon effects (I'm sorry, but there's no substitute for actually setting your actress on fire, and there never will be) and that clunky double title (did you *really* have name-check *Snakes on a Plane* too?) it's pretty alright and manages to get most of its piss in the bowl. Which is more then I can say for some movies. Or my college roommates.

Frost Bite

(2013)

Directed by Joe Davison

See, *Dead Snow*? Here's a "zombies in the snow" title that makes sense. I also would have accepted "Dead Cold", "Thaw of the Dead", and "The Winter of Our Disembowelment". Unfortunately, the rest of this one is pretty lame; it's mostly just people arguing in a tiresome fashion, until the very end when the zombies finally barge into their hidey-hole and kill everybody. (In the zombie biz, this is known as the *Day of the Dead* template.) We begin with our identification character, a hot chick who, despite being twat-deep in snow, is drinking water out of a plastic bottle. The environment thanks you, bitch. Soon two more escapees from the zombie apocalypse turn up, but they both want to rape her so she quickly cleans their clocks, moves on, and eventually hooks up with one group of survivors who are fighting tooth and nail (and gun) with another group of survivors that... *Oh my fucking god the brunette sporting the specs is so fucking fine.* Seriously, Spectacles, you take a bite out of my frost any day, and I know that doesn't make any sense but we just saw your legs and so much blood is currently rushing out of my head to support another part of my body that even the double entendre portion of my brain is shutting down. Deep breaths... Deep breaths... Okay, where was I? Meh, who cares? The scene where the broad gives the "I was supposed to live through this" speech is surprisingly poignant, and the big climax, set in a grocery store, *might* have been cool if they'd been allowed to break anything, but overall this flick is too damn talky and there aren't anywhere near enough zombies or parts where Spectacles wraps her unbelievable legs around my head while I weep for my good fortune. And in my book, at least one of those things is entirely unacceptable.

Shot, at no doubt great expense, in the state of Alaska, which is absurd. They could've gotten the same "depressing, icy wasteland" effect shooting in Toledo, Ohio. As long as they wrapped by mid-May or so.

Garden of the Dead

(1972)

Directed by John Hayes

Work farm escapees, ruthlessly riddled with bullets and buried in shallow graves, come back as axe (and rake and shovel) wielding zombies with an agenda: "We will destroy the living." Their weaknesses include a formaldehyde addiction (meh, overrated), susceptibility to light, and an inability to resist ogling pussy, but they do their fair share of damage before they're defeated, due in no small part to the fact that they are total, amped-up spazzes. Don't ever let anyone tell you that the first movie featuring fast zombies was *28 Days Later* (2002) or *Return of the Living Dead* (1985), because *Garden of the Dead* trumped them both. This movie has its flaws (no tits, no real gore, stock TV music that made me feel like I was watching *Mannix*), but there's plenty of action and it's never boring. I'd say a sequel/remake, this time set at an all-girls reform school, is definitely in order. "Garden of the Dead 2: Bush of the Dead". Now seeking investors. And before you ask, yes, I will happily cast your daughter/niece/girlfriend "...who's a really good actress, actually." She has to be willing to do topless though.

The Hanging Woman

(1973)

Directed by J. L. Merino

"If you aren't a spirit now, you soon will be..." says our main guy, pistol in hand, when he hears a noise coming from the cemetery. What he finds is a woman who was strung up after she was already dead, and the investigation begins at the home of the local grave robber/necrophiliac, where two cops discover... a cache of ladies' underwear! ("The scoundrel!" says one.) The main guy, meanwhile, inherits some property due to this weird and untimely death, and when the butler attached to the place refuses to acknowledge his authority and starts making your typical cryptic horror movie comments, the main guy immediately kicks his ass and runs him off at gunpoint! Ohmigod, I've waited *decades* to see someone deck one of those willfully obtuse horror movie servants. I cannot stress how awesome this main cat is: despite all the voodoo, mad science, Igor attacks, séances, and zombie murders going on around him he just careens through the story like he doesn't know these tropes even exist, or care how he's supposed to react to them. Making this, in a way, the *Big Lebowski* of zombie movies. The zombies don't make the scene in any major way until the last twenty minutes or so, but until then there's plenty of violence, T&A, and our main guy's cocky arrogance to keep you engaged. Probably my favorite old-school zombie movie.

Hell of the Living Dead

(1980)

Directed by Vincent Dawn

Military guys (played by Italians) are dropped into the jungle (played by stock footage) where they navigate a river (played by the ocean) to a research facility (played by an oil refinery) overrun by zombies (played by extras with greasepaint smeared all over their faces). People are eaten, zombies are popped, fingers are bitten off, eyes are gouged out (from the inside!), plus there's music stolen from *Dawn of the Dead* (1978), tits (regular and famine-impacted, *National Geographic* varieties), this classic exchange...

CHICK: "Who are they? Look at the way they walk!"

DUDE: "I can't see how many of them there are..."

CHICK: "Just look at those faces! They look like monsters!"

DUDE: "They could be drunk."

...and the industrial accident that sets the whole megilla into motion is just too fucking much: a zombie rat discovered in a supposedly sterile area gets under this tech's protective hood and starts chewing on his face (OSHA recommendations pending), initiating a zombie epidemic and prompting the department head to note "The experimental project Operation Sweet Death must be considered a complete failure." Ha ha!

Dude, you are so fired. Beginning to end, this movie is dumb, gory crap, but there's too much dead time and assing around along the way so somehow they managed to make it boring anyway. If I were the distributor, I'd chop a good twenty minutes out of this bitch, minimum. Oh, and that brunette at the very end? There would definitely be some re-shoots where she showed us her tits.

High School of the Dead

(2010)

Series Directed by Tetsuro Araki

My tolerance for foreign animation is pretty fucking low. Oh, I'll watch *Angel's Friends*, and Nazi propaganda cartoons from the 1940's, but that's pretty much it. "Japanimation" is the worst though, because they *never* know when to rein it in. I mean, a zombie apocalypse cartoon series is a perfectly serviceable idea (hell, most current zombie movies are full of cartoon zombies anyway), but the Japanese always feel the need to tack on everything and the kitchen sink too, so I fully expected a bunch of robots to eventually show up, or giant bees, or giant robot bees. But nope, as it turns out this is a straightforward cartoon series about the zombie apocalypse, the sole gimmick being that it's mostly teenage schoolgirls fighting the zombies. Which, needless to say, ups the ante to AWESOME. Story-wise it's nothing zombie fans haven't seen several hundred times before, but the fact that it's an honest-to-ass cartoon take on the concept does adds some novelty value, and there are a few cool bits (zombies that are on fire still try to come after people, a dude escapes death when a zombie can't bite through the motorcycle helmet it's wearing, the authorities plowing through zombies with a bulldozer), some good quotes ("What's wrong with you? This is armageddon, man up!"; "All these zombies and I'm gonna get killed by an Asian woman driver!"), and of course an obsessive preoccupation with tits & ass, because the Japanese have no respect for women whatsoever. It's a good show, but I do have to ask: what is with the ridiculous amount of filler in Episode 4? I swear, if you cut out all the recaps, flashbacks, credits, and *Next Week On...*'s the entire episode clocks in at maybe ten minutes. It's like one of those clip shows where Arnold, Willis, and Mr. Drummond remember various things that happened to them over the years so that they can get an extra episode in the can without paying the actors any more money. And that makes sense in a show *with* actors (because fuck actors), but this is a *cartoon* for Christ's sake. Sure, there's the voice actors, but they could've produced multiple episodes where no one spoke at all, if they'd really wanted to.

Hood of the Living Dead

(2005)

Directed by Jose and Eduardo Quiroz

Of course this movie exists.

One thing I'm tired of seeing in these movies is how they always treat someone getting a mouth full of zombie blood as a throwaway, gross-out joke. Think about it - if being bitten by a zombie turns you into a zombie, isn't it likely that swallowing an amount of zombie blood would have the same effect? Yet it never plays out that way, no matter how much blood geysers into some clown's pie hole as they stand there chainsawing a zombie while bellowing like a retard. Well in this movie, the guy who gets zombie blood in his mouth *does* turn into a zombie, endearing it to me instantly, despite the putrid acting (I'm looking at you, main guy) and an inexcusable lack of tits. The story, naturally, is the first thing that pops into your head when you hear the words "Hood of the Living Dead": an idiot scientist (is there any other kind?) uses this cell-regenerate to revive his brother after a drive-by, only for the brother to come back as a zombie, kicking off a zombie outbreak in the hood. (Oakland, to be precise, which might have been topical if this movie had been made ten years earlier.) It's not a bad little zombie flick, the only real problem being that the outbreak is relatively contained and never mushrooms to truly epic proportions. If I'd made this movie it would've featured hordes of zombies overrunning the entire hood and clashing with wave after wave of heavily-armed gang bangers, while the cops did nothing (because no white people were involved) and the local news ran a story about Justin Bieber getting a new haircut. Now there's some social commentary for you, George Romero.

Horror of the Zombies

(1974)

Directed by Amando de Ossorio

Hey, I know these guys! It's the Blind Dead, famous for riding their zombie horses in slow motion across the Spanish countryside and zeroing in on victims by listening for their heartbeats. I wonder where they got a boat? However it happened, when two chicks find their way on board the Blind Dead make short work of them, and when several additional idiots – including a blonde, a modeling agent, a thug, a meteorologist, and "Howard Tucker, the sporting goods magnate" – come looking for said chicks they're trapped there as well. Now, these clowns aren't exactly the brightest tools in the box, and with their combined skills (modeling, selling sporting goods, knowing whether it's raining or not) they couldn't fight plaque much less zombies, so you can pretty much guess how it turns out for them. The best exchange comes when the meteorologist tries to explain why they can see other boats going by, but those boats can't see them:

METEOROLOGIST: "I told you before we're in another dimension."

HOWARD TUCKER (SPORTING GOODS MAGNATE): "That's what you think!"

Eventually our dimwitted heroes do come up with a plan though: when the Blind Dead climb into their special boxes for a little nap, they toss all the boxes overboard! They probably think they're pretty clever, at least until the survivors swim to shore only to find that the Blind Dead have simply walked all the way to the beach, underwater, to get them.

Ha ha! Nice try. Blind Dead: 1, Idiots: Nothing

I Am Legend

(2007)

Directed by Francis Lawrence

Okay, I get that sometimes you have to change shit around when you turn a book into a movie. Hell, some books don't have any shower scenes in them at all! But when a book is called *I Am Legend* and the movie version is called *I Am Legend* and you leave out the part where the main guy finds out that he's legend, well, there's no other word for it except "retarded". Seriously, what slack-jawed moron made *that* call? Whoever it was, I'll bet he shits himself a lot.

So, with the entire point of the story out of the way all we're left with is a movie about the Fresh Prince of Bel-Air fighting zombies, which doesn't sound so bad until it turns out that the zombies are *goddamned cartoons*. Look, even I will admit that sometimes cartoons are your best option; there's no other way they could've done the scene where the Fresh Prince is chasing all those deer through the city with his car, for example. Well, not without pissing off PETA, anyway. But there is **NO FUCKING REASON ON EARTH** for the zombies in this movie to be cartoons, except of course Hollywood's endless fucking obsession with using cartoon effects whenever possible, no matter how crummy or fake they ultimately look.

Wake up, Hollywood - the emperor has no clothes. Not that anyone can tell, because he's a goddamned cartoon they added in post so no one is ever looking directly at him.

The amazing thing about this flick is that they still manage to pull off the occasional moment of badass. You just can't argue with the part where the Fresh Prince stumbles into that first room full of zombies, or the scene where he's forced to kill his own dog with his bare hands. It just goes to show how truly epic this movie could've been if fewer tards had been involved. But sadly, for every cool bit there's endless pathetic shit like the awful cartoon scene where the Fresh Prince is running down zombies with his SUV. For real, it looks like something out of *Grand Theft Auto*, and not even the latest one. Like *Grand Theft Auto III* or something. And what in fuck's name is with the corny-ass happy ending??? All it was missing was a goddamned rainbow. Maybe they couldn't figure out how to design a cartoon one.

I Am Omega

(2007)

Directed by Griff Furst

The last man on Earth, eh? Well, we all know what that means: no tits. The good news is that this guy lives in one of those all mod con post-apocalyptic worlds where he still has electricity, running water, and Internet service. The bad news? Zombies. Fortunately, our main guy knows kung fu, as we learn when he engages in a half-assed training scene and then beats up a defenseless fence. Heh... "defenseless fence". That's pretty funny. Anyway, eventually some more last persons on Earth show up, and as it turns out one of them is a hot chick after all. The last piece on Earth. (You know what would be a great idea for a movie? The last woman on Earth is a fat chick, but she's the only game in town so all these guys ruthlessly kill each other for her tubby love. Then, when the last cat standing makes his move, she reveals that she's a lesbian.) There are a few dumb parts (a convertible is probably not the best choice when you're planning on plowing through zombie hordes) but all-in-all this is actually a pretty decent flick. The only thing about it that pissed me off was the Alabama joke; I swear, I rewound that part at least six times and I *still* couldn't make out the punch line. Fucking enunciate, idiot.

I Eat Your Skin

(1964)

Directed by Del Tenney

A writer, his boss, and the boss's wife all travel to "Voodoo Island" where they're chased around by voodoo guys and zombies. It sounds like your typical lame, old-school zombie flick (i.e. before zombies ate people), but as it turns out this movie rocks pretty hard. First off, the writer is hilarious: he's always surrounded by hot pussy, and when one fan's irate husband shows up he just laughs at her when her husband kicks her in the ass. This guy is awesome. His boss is pretty cool too - he convinces the writer to go to Voodoo Island in the first place by telling him it's full of hot, virgin pussy, and he forces his own wife to tag along by threatening to cancel all her credit cards. See, that's how one comes to be the boss: by knowing how to motivate people. Once things really get rolling a zombie decapitates a guy with a machete, another zombie walks into an airplane propeller while carrying a box of "Explosive" (BAM!), a native is shot in the chest with a flare gun, and in the end the whole damn island explodes. Apparently this movie has a pretty bad reputation but I can't imagine why. There's nothing not to like here. Thumbs up.

(Er, I can say "thumbs up" without Roger Ebert suing me, now that he's dead, right?)

Insane in the Brain

(2007)

Directed by Chad Hendricks

Afro-sporting zombies that endlessly scream "Brains! More brains!" (and I do mean endlessly; it could be a drinking game, except you'd die) crash this pimp's ho-down (heh) and the local drive-in, but they don't actually eat brains, so why they go on and on about them is a complete mystery. Newsflash: just saying "Brains! More brains!" over and over and over again isn't funny. And neither are the other "jokes" in this movie, which include farting, black people being stereotypes, farting, and farting. I can just picture director/writer/editor/farter Chad Hendricks lounging around his house, laughing hysterically as he farts and shits his pants all day long. He probably sticks his finger in it and smells it too. In the end the zombies can only be stopped with rubber bullets, because they're all brothers, see, and brothers are afraid of rubbers. Ha ha! It's funny because at least it wasn't yet another character farting. Okay, to be fair there are a *few* good gags (three, to be precise), and one nice pair of tits, but the other 99% of this movie is pretty wretched, and if you can get through it without being embarrassed for yourself, Chad Hendricks, and the whole of the human race, you're a stronger man than me. Stronger smelling at least, because if you think this movie is funny, you probably just farted.

I Was a Teenage Mummy

(1962)

Directed by Ralph C. Bluemke

Okay, what the curse-defying fuck? This was made by a bunch of little kids! In the 1960's! I guess you have to give 'em props for making it in the first place, but when one of them drags it out of its box in the basement thirty years later, adds a bunch of dumb jokes, and puts the damn thing out on video I think things have gone a bit too far. Seriously, buddy - it's time to move on. The new shit our... er, what's the opposite of "benefactor"? Anyway, the new shit he added is unbelievably lame, but there's still some hilarious stuff here, like when the mummy kidnaps the main chick (who's pretty damn hot for a thirteen-year-old) and nobody even bothers to rescue her, or when one of the characters gets completely shitfaced at a party and his buddy, who's stone sober, lets him drive anyway. I can't imagine why anybody would want to watch this unless they were actually in it (and probably not even then), but frankly it's no worse than *The Mummy Returns*, and *somebody* in the 1960's had to make a teenage mummy movie, even if it was a bunch of bored kids who hadn't discovered smoking dope yet.

I wonder if any of them are dead now?

I Was a Teenage Mummy

(1992)

Directed by Christopher C. Frieri

Wow, from a teenage mummy movie made in the 1960's and dusted off in the 1990's, to a teenage mummy movie made in the 1990's but pretending to be from the 1960's. I guess it's true: the more things change, they more they remain utterly retarded. The retarded begins when some not-so-juvenile delinquents beat up this fez-sporting camel jockey, then shove his head in the toilet. It turns out he kinda deserved it though, because he's a total creep: instead of going out and getting himself a gun like a respectable pussy, he grabs this hottie off the street, knocks her out, dry humps her for a while, turns her into a killer mummy, and then sends *her* to waste the bullies. It's gory enough in a cheesy sort of way (face bashed in with a rock, arm ripped off, dipshit decapitated) and most of the chicks are surprisingly doable, but since this is trying to pass itself off as a movie from the early sixties there aren't any tits on display, which is too bad because the mummy and the tramp she kills at the very end are both particularly fine and, just out of personal curiosity, I really wanted to know what their tits looked like. Pretty fucking awesome, I would imagine.

I Was a Zombie for the FBI

(1982)

Directed by Marius Penczner

According to William Poundstone's amazing book *Big Secrets*, W. W. Clements, former CEO of Dr Pepper, once said that he used to worry about someone stealing their secret formula: "Then I got to thinking. Why would anyone go to all that trouble just to produce another Dr Pepper? Then I quit worrying." Obviously he never saw this movie, where aliens steal the formula for the world's most popular soft drink and use it to produce their own competing brand so that... Okay, I didn't catch exactly why they're doing this, but "to take over the world" and "to increase the value of our stock" are probably two good guess. With aliens, a flying weapons-grade sphere, and a crazy monster on hand it sounds like it's just a few dwarfs and one ponytailed douche away from being a *Phantasm* sequel, but it's really more of a quirky cult movie, and by "cult" movie, of course, I mean "a movie that only a small subset of people will like because it's nowhere near as good as its wild – and dishonest – title would suggest". See, no one in this flick actually becomes a zombie for the FBI, or even because of them. Instead, it's a bunch of hapless small-townsfolk who are zombified, by the aliens, to serve as cheap labor in their soda plant. As a result there's no gut-munching zombie gore, but there are some legitimately funny bits, like when we briefly see the secret formula which contains, among other things, soy sauce, peanut butter, and river water. My favorite thing about this flick though is that a lot of the action takes place in a town called Pleasantville, making this, in my opinion, the least heavy-handed movie set in a town named Pleasantville ever made. Heh. I did like that Beatles song Fiona Apple covered for the *Pleasantville* (1998) soundtrack though. Did I even tell you about my idea for a zombie sitcom starring her as the... Okay, okay. Jesus. I won't bring it up again.

Just Say No

(2011)

Directed by Abiel Bruhn and John Rocco

So, the urban legend goes that there was once this chemical, designed specifically to kill marijuana, that would make recently dead bodies twitch around if they were exposed to it. Something to do with stimulating the nervous system or some such shit. Anyway, extrapolating from this, they made at least one movie where marijuana defoliant turned people into zombies, and thirty years later movies like *Just Say No* and *Evil Weed* (2010) are still turning people into zombies and monsters via tainted ganja, no doubt convinced that they were the first ones to dream up the idea. The doped-up dead this time include our main dealer (a typical Joe Sixdork who I immediately hated) and several of his friends and customers, who keep right on smoking the bad weed even though it's *clearly* turning them into zombies. And they say pot isn't addictive. ("It's not *addictive*. It's *habit-forming*." -Every annoying hippie ever) Once the splatter hits the fan this flick is pretty gory, but there's no tits, the acting is hella shitty, the dumb script was obviously dashed off over a weekend by drunken imbeciles, and their pathetic attempts at originally are limited solely to setting the story at Christmas (wow, just like *It's a Wonderful Life*), and a lame *That '70's Show* reference. The only, and I mean only, positive here is Brittany Cerra as the chick who dies off camera after everyone abandons her.

Chivalry really is dead. Anyway, she is beyond fine, and I think she'll go far if she just stays away from these dope-smoking zombie movies.

King of the Zombies

(1941)

Directed by Jean Yarbrough

A black guy and two white guys are flying to the "Ba-hey-mas", but something goes wrong and they end up crashing on an unidentified island. This doctor who happens to live on the island tells them that they're welcome to chill at his pad until help arrives, but weird shit starts to go down and they eventually learn that the doctor is really a Nazi spy who's turning everyone into zombies! The black guy spends the vast majority of this movie running around terrified, but who can blame him? There's Nazi zombies all over the place - he *should* be terrified. The two white guys, on the other hand, are complete imbeciles: they can't pronounce "Bahamas", they don't recognize German when they hear it (even though Germany was kind of in the news in 1941), and they don't believe anything the black guy tells them even though he's right every single time. Stupid crackers. On the plus side this does feature Nazis *and* zombies, which is a pretty unbeatable combination. I know these old movies where the white people are intentionally portrayed as ignorant buffoons aren't considered "politically correct" these days, but if you can get past that, this really is an okay flick.

Land of the Dead

(2005)

Directed by George A. Romero

So, zombies have overrun the Earth, excluding one city that's safely nestled behind these two rivers. Everyone who lives in this city is constantly pissing & moaning though, the zombie apocalypse not being enough drama for these fools, and eventually one of them completely loses his shit, steals some sort of supertruck, and threatens to shoot missiles at the city if they don't give him five million dollars. Okay, let's stop and think about this for a moment. The whole world is ended. Besides burning it to keep warm, what is this guy possibly going to do with five million dollars? Hell, he might as well ask for five *trillion* dollars. What the fuck, right? Seriously, what a complete fucking moron. Meanwhile, it suddenly dawns on the dead (heh) that they can just walk *through* the rivers, so they stroll into town and eat everybody. From a "making any damn sense" standpoint this movie is utterly hopeless, but there is plenty of gore, a midget sporting a purple suit and a cowboy hat is shot in the head, and the ladies are fine as fuck, especially featured babe Asia Argento (one of the hottest chicks since the dawn of time, in case you didn't know, fag). We never see Asia naked though, which is odd because if you look her up on the Internet she seems to be naked pretty much all the time. Since she is far and away the best thing here, her sudden prudishness really hurts this movie's rewatchability, assuming that's even a word. Which, my dictionary informs me, it is not. Which means you've failed yet again, *Land of the Dead*, you dumb piece of crap.

Last of the Living

(2009)

Directed by Logan McMillan

Three of the most careless jokers imaginable are somehow still alive after the zombie apocalypse, and they spend all their time looting stores that inexplicably still have power. That's right, the people who made this movie have that unique form of tunnel vision (generally a result of stupidity) that allows them to forget that if everyone on Earth suddenly stopped doing their jobs, then shit like remotely generated electricity and curbside trash service would no longer exist. It's one of the main reasons why I am so over the zombie apocalypse. Can't the world be overrun by some other kind of monster for a change? What about, say, a werewolf apocalypse? Everything would be business as usual most of the time, but come the full moon and wham! It's a goddamned free-for-all. How cool would that be? And, for the rest of the month, we'd still have Internet service. This flick does introduce one interesting angle - the idea that the zombies can be, well, cured. Of course, this means that they're not really zombies, *per se*, just a bunch of really, really sick people still capable of walking around. This lends a pretty distasteful air to the scenes where our main guys are gallivanting about, gleefully bashing their heads in with baseball bats and eviscerating them with circular saws. What's next, dicks? Nail gun rampage through the intensive care unit?

Legion of the Dead

(2005)

Directed by Paul Bales

Bruce Boxliner and the kid from *Gremlins* (1984) are forced to contend with several mummies unleashed on southern California, where, as all movie fans know, 90% of everything takes place. The queen of the mummies is a sexy little number who repeatedly shows us her tits, faces are melted off, a chick's spine is forcibly removed (Now she's ready to date me. Ha ha!), a heart is torn out (been there), a mummy is decapitated with a fire extinguisher (you know, because fire extinguishers have those sharp edges), one guy's brains leak out after he takes an axe to the noggin, a face is gnawed on, and there's a great closing line. Plus rampant abuse of the editing software's orange filter, and a girl named "Kevin".

All in all, it's passable entertainment.

Lost Tapes "Zombies"

(2010)

Directed by Douglas Segal

I suppose it was inevitable that the godawful hand-held *Blair Witch* lost & found footage style of making horror movies would be applied to TV eventually, but the result – a weird, transparently fake "reality" series about monsters – is actually pretty good, and their inevitable zombie installment beats the pants off the "official" lost & found footage zombie movie (*Diary of the Dead*) hands down. It opens with a zombie attack at Mardi Gras, prompting the arrival of a private security firm, who are called in by police because... Er, actually the police think they're dealing with a standard murder here, so I have no idea why they called in a private firm. I guess, like most cops, they're just lazy. Anyway, the security team (which includes one notable hottie) arrives to round up the primary suspect, rumored to be squatting in an abandoned building. Just like every other resident of New Orleans post-Katrina! Ha ha! It's funny because it's true. Anyway, after creeping around the place for a while they're attacked by zombies, and naturally the token rookie is bitten and has to be put down (fucking noob). It's a fun show, and this installment is actually kinda scary, but I really have to ask: why is a program like this airing on *Animal Planet???* They started running it around they same time they trotted out their completely non-animal-oriented ghost show *The Haunted,* and if this keeps up they could very well become the next TLC, which started out as The Learning Channel, embraced shows about UFOs and Atlantis to briefly became The Loony Channel, and eventually discovered Honey Boo Boo and her chromosome-hoarding family at which point they finally settled on being The Loser Channel. If Animal Planet continues to follow TLC's trajectory, they'll be airing graphic bestiality shows starring washed-up celebrities by 2025. I will admit, I'm kinda looking forward to the day when Perez Hilton is reduced to blowing old goats. Like he doesn't already.

Lust in the Mummy's Tomb

(2002)

Directed by William Hellfire

This movie begins with officially-recognized sex goddess Misty Mundae taking a *really* long shower, and while that's hardly a bad thing I'm not in the shower this long when I'm *thinking* about Misty Mundae. Seriously, movie, get on with it already.

So, for some reason Misty's pop has a mummy stored in the den, and it just happens to be sporting the biggest goddamn mummy chubby you've ever seen, so Misty decides to hop on board and go for a little ride down the Nile. Okay, I've seen a few pornos in my time so I think I know a thing or two about women, and given all the options available in the refrigerator alone I really can't imagine any girl going for the mummy. Correct me if I'm wrong, ladies. Misty seems to have a pretty good time though, at least until the damn thing actually comes to life. (Ha! "Comes to life." That joke never gets old.) Now, I don't doubt for a second that Misty Mundae could fuck a dead guy back to life, but why is she so upset when he suddenly wants a second helping? Once you've screwed a 3000-year-old corpse – on purpose – what could possibly happen next that you wouldn't be into? Whatever her logic, Misty's not having it, so she tricks the mummy into unraveling himself and that's the end of him. It seems like that should be the end of the movie too, but Misty isn't done yet - next she dykes it out with the mummy's former girlfriend, who, I'm sorry to report, is fucking *rogue*. Seriously, she's so goddamned heinous that I can't even do an image grab from the DVD to show you how ugly she is; every time I try, I just get a pop-up that says "No." How does someone that hideous even get *into* porn? The only thing I can figure is that blackmail must be involved. Maybe she has pictures of one of the producers fucking her.

The Mad

(2007)

Directed by John Kalangis

For the first half hour or so this seems like it might be a pretty good zombie movie. The characters act and sound like real human beings; it's not full of stupid, idiot mistakes; and the chicks are all especially scrumptious. After a while though it's painfully obvious that a good 50% of the scenes and dialogue are just there to tread water, which is even more pathetic when you realize that this flick is pretty damn short to begin with. I especially lost patience with the main guy repeatedly bringing up the band he used to be in. Like I told Eddie Vedder: if I wanna hear about your stupid fucking band, I'll let you know, and trust me, I won't be letting you know. The bit where a decapitated head bounces right into one of those novelty place-your-face carnival cutouts finally rockets this one into *Oh, fuck you* territory, and the climax forgets all about the zombies to concentrate on a confrontation with a couple of rednecks. Parts of it are gory, and, as I said, the girls are hot, but in the end this is just another lazy, insultingly stupid movie that thinks I'm indiscriminate enough to accept a lazy, insultingly stupid movie like this one. Which I'm not. Unless there's nudity in it.

Miner's Massacre

(2002)

Directed by John Carl Buechler

This whiner 49er is pissing in his britches (colloquially, I mean) because some guy found his leprechaun gold, so he rises from the dead and kills the bastard. Then the guy's friends show up and the zombie kills them too. He doesn't fuck around, either, dragging his feet and killing them one or two at a time as they sneak off to piss or have sex - he just marches into their camp and starts offing 'em right in front of each other. This does serve to speed up our story a bit, which is a plus because this movie *fucking sucks*. The sole hot chick – in case you have worse taste in women than me, she's the super bitchy one wearing the red top – is decapitated without ever showing us her tits, and even though everyone seems to spend plenty of time screwing all we ever see are a couple of bare asses, and one of those belongs to a dude. Even the part where the undead 49er gets his comeuppance is lame - instead of suffering a richly gory demise, he's blown up after falling onto a pile of dynamite, dying quickly and cleanly like so many cartoon coyotes before him. If there's ever an Academy Award for lame (and Lord knows there should be), this movie should receive the first one, to be accepted by the actress who played the bitchy chick in the red top. Also she'll be naked when she accepts it, and afterwards she'll give me an epic hummer in the limo on our way to pick up Ke$ha for that threesome.

Mortuary

(2005)

Directed by Tobe Hooper

Damn, Tasha Yar hit the hag wall like she was fired out of a rocket. No wonder she buys a mortuary in this movie - she probably needs continuous access to embalming fluid and spare parts just to perform general upkeep. And not that I care, but don't you need some sort of degree to be a mortician? The first time we see her working on a stiff (heh) she looks like she's trying to learn as she goes, using a book she got out of the library. Maybe this scene is supposed to be comedic. Ha ha! Dead bodies! Anyway, it seems that there's an unzoned sarlacc pit located beneath the cemetery next door, and it's spitting out this fungus that turns people into tar-puking zombies. Except sometimes when it doesn't. Oh, and there's a retard who occasionally throws people into the pit, but he's not a zombie. At least, I don't think he is. Truth be told, it's all kind of confusing, but before long the fungus has clearly infected a decent portion of the cast – including Tasha, a douchebag who never got the memo about grunge being a) over and b) a complete hoax, both of said douchebag's girlfriends (hey, it's a small town - there's only so many douchebags to go around), the unbelievably irritating sheriff, and a few random corpses – all of whom/which soon become zombies. It's a stupid, shitty movie made by and for assholes that makes zero fucking sense and doesn't care if you enjoy watching it or not, which you won't. In short, another typical entry from Tobe "*Texas Chain Saw Massacre* and nothing else of any consequence, ever" Hooper.

The Mummy

(1932)

Directed by Karl Freund

Old mummy movies are almost always fucking lame. The best you can hope for is that the mummy will manage to strangle somebody before he accidentally sets himself on fire, falls into the river, or just dies of old age. This mummy movie is particularly bad though, because the mummy, in his true form at least, barely even makes an appearance! Instead, he spends most of his time disguised as a regular guy with bad skin, which means he's about as frightening as one of those old bags who spends all day smoking poolside at the hotel, bad-mouthing her dead husband and chugging watered-down cosmopolitans. Actually I'd give the edge to the old bag, because she's way more likely to buy you tequila shots until you're drunk enough to consider fucking her. And it just so happens that the mummy is thinking along these same lines re: the main chick in this movie, except his plan involves plying her with a magical spell instead of free booze. See how that all came together? Nice, right?

The mummy and Mrs. Greenberg, I mean Janice, aren't the only weirdos on the prowl (fuck you, she actually looks pretty good for 56, and she says she's getting some work done really, really soon). At one point the main chick faints and our main guy, whom she's never met before, takes it upon himself to carry her back to his crib. Here's the conversation they have when she comes to:

MAIN CHICK: "How did I get here?"

MAIN GUY: "We brought you here, Father and I."

Yeah, that's not creepy. Meanwhile all the "mummy" does is sneak around, stare at people, and try to cast his ridiculous spells. He reminds me of my high school girlfriend's mom. The only decent part of this movie is at the very end, when the main chick is all decked out like an Egyptian princess. Chicks dressed as Egyptian princesses are so fucking hot.

The Mummy's Hand

(1940)

Directed by Christy Cabanne

Two annoying idiots find a map pinpointing the location of an ancient Egyptian tomb, so they round up a few friends and hurry off to ransack the place. This evil priest wants to put the kibosh on their plans though (remember kids, if you aren't white, attempting to preserve your country's cultural and historical treasures is *evil*), so he uses some magical juice to bring a mummy to life and orders it to kill the lot of them. Now even the mummy, the slowest monster ever (with the possible exception of the gelatinous cube), should be able to make short work of these halfwits, but apparently he needs a juice fix at surprisingly short regular intervals to stay mobile, so instead of taking care of business he spends most his time stumbling aimlessly around, looking for another drink. They could've just made a movie about my dad. In the end some of the magic juice is spilled, so while the mummy's down on his hands and knees lapping it off the floor like the junkie loser he is the good guys easily set him on fire and that's the end of him. Nice job, you fucking addict. This movie sucks.

The Mummy's Tomb

(1942)

Directed by Harold Young

So, thirty years later, the evil Egyptian cultural curator from *The Mummy's Hand* sends his protégé, with the mummy in tow, to kick the next generation's ass. Why he even deems this necessary is beyond me, but you know how these people are with their curses: they have to play it out *just so,* and they're never happy unless everyone who's even peripherally involved gets their predetermined helping of grief. It's so OCD. How the new guy sneaks an entire mummy through Customs is left to the imagination (now *that* would be an interesting movie), but he pulls it off and pretty soon the mummy is roaming the suburbs of Massachusetts, choking people out. After the protégé feeds it a potion made from a *very specific* number of magical leaves, of course. Like I said, OCD. At first nobody knows *what* the fuck is going on, but they know it ain't normal. "Witchcraft Revived in New England?" asks one newspaper headline. (Also: "Victim Slugged, Robbed by Thugs". That's great.) They figure it out soon enough though, and a club-bearing, torch-wielding, hat-wearing mob confronts the protégé, at which point he produces a gun and tries to cap the final person on his list. Okay, hold the phone. He can do that? Why didn't he just shoot them all in the first place then???

It would've been a lot easier than dealing with this endlessly convoluted leaf and mummy nonsense. I'll tell ya, man: OC fucking *D*.

The Mummy's Ghost

(1944)

Directed by Reginald Le Borg

At the end of *The Mummy's Tomb* they cornered the mummy in a spacious New England home and then burned the entire building to the ground, much to the chagrin, no doubt, of the person who owned the place. Afterward the main guy (defined, in this case, as the only guy who hadn't been killed) married his girl and they lived happily ever after ("Romance Scores Triumph Over Terror Reign"). You can't keep a good monster down though (Or this one either. Ha ha!), so somehow the mummy pops back to not being a tiny pile of ashes and goes on the rampage again. I kid because it's stupid, but truth be told this is far and away the best of the old-school mummy movies: the mummy smashes right through fences and walls, is attacked by a hound dog, busts up a museum, takes out this backdoor bro who tries to cock block him, and racks up a fairly decent body count, including the main chick! (Looks like romance doesn't score a triumph this time. Tough break, new main guy.) I also liked the fact that no one wasted any time blaming all this trouble on anything but the mummy. It's about damn time these people showed some sense. All this plus a little dog that may or may not be named "Penis", and a part where this old lady almost falls into a pit they dug to trap the mummy. Oh, if only that would've happened. Talk about hilarious.

The Mummy's Curse

(1944)

Directed by Leslie Goodwins

When last we saw the mummy (*The Mummy's Ghost*) he was sinking into a bog after rampaging through Massachusetts and being run down by the local townsfolk, but now he's buried in a swamp in Cajun country? At first I thought maybe he swam through a really long underground tunnel, but that doesn't fit the facts because everyone on hand remembers the end of the previous movie and it's abundantly clear from the way they talk about it that it went down nearby. Maybe those townsfolk chased him further than I thought? Of course the simplest explanation is usually the correct one, so I think it's clear what's really happened here: in the 25 years that passed between the events in these two movies there was another Civil War, and this time Louisiana won. That amazing turn of events aside, this whole mummy business is getting pretty played out; the guy who wrote this script must have gotten *so* tired of typing the word "lumbers". And the human characters don't show a lot of sense. I mean, a beautiful, amnesic chick strolls out of the bayou and not one person thinks to take her to the hospital, or contact the authorities? When you stop to think about it, it's pretty sketchy. They all probably belong to a white slavery ring or something, and they're just waiting for their chance to sell her into sexual bondage. Fucking degenerates. Seriously, what's this country coming to? This isn't the United Republic of Louisiana that I grew up in.

The Mummy

(1959)

Directed by Terence Fisher

This is one of those movies where everyone is veddy, veddy British and no matter how much crazy, evil, supernatural shit goes down their only reaction is to be mildly annoyed. My favorite example of this is when the mummy suddenly bursts through a set of doors and goes straight for this bloke's throat. The guy just stands there with this "I say, how peculiar" look on his face, like this sort of thing almost never happens to him, and it's a bit of a bloody nuisance that it's happening right now, because he's got things to do, don't you know.

Now, unlike the mummy in your classic mummy movies (in this case, "classic" just means "old") this mummy doesn't dilly-dally around when he's got a job to do - he can actually *move*. For some reason though the cat pulling his ~~strings~~ bandages only sends him after one person at a time, which isn't very efficient and serves to drag the story out a lot longer that necessary. It isn't gory either, and while the sole chick on hand is okay, she's nothing to break out the twelve-dollar bottle of wine for, unless you plan on drinking the entire bottle yourself, in which case you're probably looking at a solid 7, max. Oh, and speaking of the chick, it was epically weak for them to wait until the movie was a good two-thirds of the way over before they suddenly pulled the old "Hey, she looks just like the mummy's true love!" angle out of their asses. There is one hilarious scene where the main cat and the bad guy have one of those polite, James Bond-style meetings where they're slyly threatening and insulting each other, but when the best part of a horror movie is talking, you know something went wrong somewhere.

The Mummy

(1997)

Directed by Jeffrey Obrow

This chick's pop is being hassled by the mummy (it lives in his basement, behind an old mattress), so she asks her pussy-whipped ex-boyfriend for help. Now, allowing yourself to be roped into your ex's picayune little crises is almost never a good idea, but at first it seems like it could work out okay for this guy, because the dad's deliriously hot, leggy little maid practically throws herself at him the minute he makes the scene. Seriously, we are talking some blue label trim here, and since his ex ain't so bad either, if he can finagle a threesome out of this it might even be worth taking on *two* mattress mummies. Predictably enough though, that's not how it plays out. Instead, he's knocked unconscious, the black guy from the *Iron Eagle* movies kicks the shit out of him, and, worst of all, he has this horrible nightmare in which he appears to have gotten laid, but then it turns out he didn't. Oh, and his friend is electrocuted in a phone booth. It all sounds exciting enough, to the layman at least, but in practice it's pretty lame, as befits a flick featuring the kind of sorry-ass mummy who limits his rampage to one house and the nearest phone booth. There's only two good things about this floater: the poppin' fresh maid, and the ex-girlfriend in tight, plaid pants. Too bad they never dyke out.

The Mummy and the Curse of the Jackals

(1969)

Directed by Oliver Drake

The Mummy and the Curse of the Jackass (heh) opens with some decent surf music, but it's all downhill after that. Our main guy has a mummy and an ancient Egyptian princess (the latter in near-mint condition!) stashed in his basement, but they come bundled with a curse and before you know it he's turning into a werejackal (which is just like a werewolf... except more of a pussy, I guess). Later the princess pops back to life, so he buys her some clothes, teaches her how to put on a bra (bastard) and takes her to dinner, only to have her mack all over his buddy before the dessert cart even arrives! Bitch has been in the 20th century for less than 48 hours and already she's a typical American whore. The main guy turns into the werejackal again, the princess knocks herself out walking into a door, the mummy shows up and carries her off, the mummy and the werejackal fight, and finally Egyptian goddess/ part-time superheroine Isis possesses the buddy and, through him, takes charge of the situation, putting this entire crew of pussy-whipped dipshits permanently at the princess's beck and call. Now if our story had ended here, maybe with the mummy, the jackal, and the other guy (I believe he said he was a "junior chemical engineer") running a train on the princess, then all this foolishness might have been worth it, but that's not what happens. Instead, the main dude's old history professor arrives to help the cops put an end to the, er, horror ("We can't just stand by and let a 4000-year-old mummy and a jackal man take over the city."), which must somehow throw the monsters' whole plan (whatever it was, exactly) out of whack because suddenly the mummy and the jackal are fighting again and the princess just keels over and disintegrates for absolutely no reason. None of it makes any Ra-damned sense, which would be okay if we at least got to see the princess's tits, but we don't, not even during the nerve-wracking bra scene. The only part of this dumb movie I liked was when the front porch railing fell off the main guy's house. "Boy, what a place!" his buddy says. I don't know why, but that really cracked me up.

The Mummy Lives

(1993)

Directed by Gerry O'Hara

Wow, starring Tony Curtis. Duh. *The Mummy Lives* opens with an astrology lesson, which would be a lot more appropriate if housewives who flunked out of high school were the primary target audience for mummy movies. I'd like to say it gets better, but it doesn't. The questionable horror begins, as you might expect, with the discovery of a mummy. The mummy comes back to life and transforms into Tony Curtis, but no one seems to notice that the mummy is missing or questions what, exactly, Tony Curtis is doing there, so everyone just goes about their business while Tony Curtis hangs around, threatening and insulting everybody. Why doesn't anyone tell him to get lost? Finally he starts killing people, but it's all pretty weak and frankly I could barely keep my eyes open, and it was like 3 o'clock in the afternoon. And I was on coke. The *really* frustrating thing though is that, concurrent to this, the main chick is having all these wild nightmares about a mummified cat coming to life, and waking up in bed next to a mummy, but the movie never develops any of this! Are you kidding me? Hell, just one death via mummy cat would have *doubled* this movie's entertainment value, by at least a factor of ten. And just imagine all the avenues the whole waking-up-next-to-a-mummy scenario could've explored. I mean, did our hapless heroine drink too many Old Fashioneds and go home with the mummy of her own volition, or did he have to slip her some ancient Egyptian mickey before he could violate her the way her friends violated his tomb? Seriously, what moron decided that mummy date rape and a mummy cat on the rampage were less interesting than listening to Tony Curtis talk shit? Whoever it was, they really needs to get their priorities straight.

Tony Curtis sucks.

The Mummy's Shroud

(1967)

Directed by John Gilling

You know what the problem with mummies is? They only have one axe to grind: archeologists, archeologists, archeologists. You almost never meet a mummy with a grudge against cobblers, or dentists, or even the Jews. And what's worse, while the real world is apparently full of sexy female physicists (Zoë Hatherell), sexy female entomologists (Kristie Reddick), and sexy female forensic metallurgists (Jennifer Hooper McCarty) I have yet to meet a sexy female archeologist. Maybe that's why the male archeologists in these movies are always dragging their young, female assistants off to some Ra-forsaken desert with them. Even if she's no great shakes (like, say, the dame in this flick) it beats trying to gerbil yourself with a scorpion.

At any rate, this mummy movie is surprisingly chintzy. We hardly even see the mummy during the first half, and when we do he's just lying there in his sar-coffin-case. Hell, I could see that at the fucking history museum, if I knew (or cared) where it was. Instead, they waste our time with chit-chat, arguing, press conferences, and a (supposedly) comedic idiot who's big gag is cleaning a room and then sweeping all the dirt under the carpet. Are you fucking kidding me? That joke was fossilized before the Earth cooled, and this is what they think we want to see in lieu of, oh, I dunno, maybe more killer mummy? Not that the parts where the mummy *is* being proactive are any better. The worst has to be the scene where this chump who's been defenestrated by the mummy lands in a watering trough/public urinal and blood just starts *gushing* out of these hidden pumps that are nowhere near the body. I'm not sure if the actor missed his mark or the special effects guy missed his mark, but either way it's pretty damned bush-league.

Or who knows, maybe we're supposed to assume he landed on a cat.

Night of the Dead: "Leben Tod"

(2006)

Directed by Eric Forsberg

Rampaging frog puppets, mannequins hit by cars, hilariously fake medical procedures... If you're looking for dumb, you came to the right movie. I'm not even sure what country it's supposed to be taking place in - all the signs are in English, but half of the characters are speaking high school German. (Incidentally, moviemakers, I've been to Germany and they don't say *schnell* as often as you seem to think they do.) Of course it doesn't really matter where this flick takes place, since sucking shit is universal. My biggest issue is with the zombies' ability to launch surprise attacks against victims who are obviously staring right at them. Listen and learn, fuckwads who made this movie: the fact that your *audience* can't see something off-frame doesn't automatically mean that your *characters* can't see it, and unless these zombies are beaming down from the starship Enterprise or bursting through the floor like the WCW's Sting there is *no way* some of these attacks could have gone off. You're either inconceivably retarded or you think I am, and either way I've got no time for you. The movie's gory, the main chick is pretty cute, and there are some tits, but in yet another boneheaded move the hottest girls in the cast have all been squandered as zombie extras! You imbecilic fucking cakeheads... If a hot chick wants to be in your movie, *you cast her as a hot chick*. Not a zombie. Not a nun. *A hot chick*. It's the role she was born to play. Jesus.

Night of the Living Dead 3D

(2006)

Directed by Jeff Broadstreet

The original *Night of the Living Dead* was a wicked-ass movie for its time, but the whole "trapped in a building by zombies" angle is so played out that yet another remake of this flick – in lame-ass 3-D yet – strikes me as a colossal waste of time. Fortunately, the people who did make *Night of the Living Dead 3D* realized this too and changed the story considerably, so I was willing to give it a chance. And at first it ain't bad: the main chick is way cute, the zombies look fantastic, and there's tits (medium quality) and even some full-frontal. UNfortunately, there's also a smattering of horrible cartoon effects, no intensity at all, annoying characters (the bald funeral director, played by that actor who's been thoroughly typecast as the treacherous dick, is especially irritating), and a dumb-as-dirt explanation for the zombie outbreak. Overall it's more bad than good, but let's face it, so is a lot of shit, including your marriage, and I think a lot more people would be okay with *Night of the Living Dead 3D* if they hadn't made the fatal misstep of calling it "Night of the Living Dead" in the first place. See, it's always a bad idea to name something mediocre after something people have a lot of affection for, which is why I finally threw in the towel regarding my diarrhea-prone Pomeranian "Princess Di" and had her put to sleep. (Although, on reflection, I probably could've just changed her name.) They should have gone with something that evokes the title "Night of the Living Dead" without actually using it, like "Curse of the Living Dead" (which a character in this movie actually says at one point) or "Assault of the Living Dead" or "Tits of the Living Dead". Hell, there's no way people wouldn't get behind a movie called "Tits of the Living Dead". Or, since they insist on bludgeoning us over the head with a dumb, wonky explanation for the zombie epidemic, how about "Causation of the Living Dead"? Regardless, put the original out of your mind and you just might end up liking *Night of the Living Dead 3D*. Probably not though.

Night of the Tripping Dead

(1968/2007)

Produced by G4 TV

Okay, so some stool-hurlers took a copy of *Night of the Living Dead* (the original) and added "funny" dialogue and sound effects. Here's a breakdown of their comedic brilliance:

- Pot "jokes": 6
- Poop "jokes": 0
- Fart "jokes": 7
- Dick "jokes": 4
- Fag "jokes": 24
- Actual funny jokes: 0

The sad part is that I compiled the above list before I even watched this; all I had to do was fill in the numbers. No ESP or psychic links necessary: for some reason the people who produce these things are *always* obsessed with poop, smoking pot, and cock. I don't know what they do on their days off, but whatever it is, you can count me out. What's truly pathetic is that this isn't even the first "comedic" voiceover that's been applied to this flick. (Another one is called *Night of the Day of the Dawn of the Son of the Bride of the Return of the Revenge of the Terror of the Attack of the Evil, Mutant, Alien, Flesh-Eating, Hellbound, Crawling, Zombified, Living-Dead Part II in*

Shocking 2-D. So witty!) Honestly, how much fucking demand can there be for different versions of *Night of the Living Dead* with farting dubbed in? It's dumbfounding.

Night of the Zombies II

(1981)

Directed by Joel M. Reed

All right, this ain't no goddamned *Night of the Zombies II*, because there was never any *Night of the Zombies I*. There *was* a completely unrelated *Night of the Zombies* that came out the year previous to this one, but these days that movie is known as *Hell of the Living Dead* so there's no way it could be confused with *Night of the Zombies*, which is this movie, AKA *Night of the Zombies II*. It's kind of like how the original *Dawn of the Dead* was called *Zombie* in Europe, and then they made a *Zombie 2* over there which is just known as *Zombie 1* in the US.

God **damn** my head hurts. Stupid fucking zombie movies.

So, two guys are putzing around in the middle of nowhere when some zombies show up and... shoot them. That's right, they don't tear them to shreds and then lovingly fondle their guts, they just *shoot* them. Dickish, sure, but it seems, I dunno, kinda pedestrian, don't you think? Regardless, some stock footage of the Pentagon quickly sends Elliot Gould lookalike "Nick" to investigate, and much trouble of the sub-sub-sub-James Bond variety follows as ~~super~~ spy Nick attacks this case like a hebe Harry Palmer, i.e. by making spy work seem as boring as humanly possible. It's doubly boring, in fact, since we, the audience, already know that the mystery is zombies, making all this nonsense about as suspenseful as the outcome of a Globetrotters/Generals game. Eventually Nick manages to infiltrate the zombies, actual World War Part 2 soldiers – ours *and* theirs – who have been hiding out in the wilderness, running regular maneuvers, and no doubt telling each other the same tiresome stories and jokes over and over again for 35 years now. And yet they don't notice a stranger suddenly appearing in their midst? It's all so fucking dumb, and I haven't even gotten to the part where it's revealed that the zombies are half vegetable. Hey, maybe that could be their new tagline: "Half Nazi... Half Vegetable... ALL Zombie!"

Okay, maybe not.

Oasis of the Zombies

(1982)

Directed by A. M. Frank

Three guys and a girl are looking for six million dollars worth of Nazi gold supposedly buried under this remote oasis, never mind that it's guarded by Nazi zombies who eat the fuck out of anyone who comes nosing around. Here's the weird part though: we always hear someone playing a washing board right before the zombies attack. If these were redneck zombies that might make sense, but Nazis hardly ever played the washing board. As zombie movies go this isn't particularly gory, and we're only treated to one pair of tits, which might just be the smallest tits in the world (except for Jessica's), but there is tons of hilarious dialogue. For example:

DICKHEAD: "Six million dollars. The girl doesn't count so that makes two million each the way I figure it."

Or how about this revealing bit of insanity, when the zombies finally attack:

LUNATIC: "Let's get some bottles and make Molotov cocktails - like in school!"

Then there's the old guy who stumbles out of the desert rambling incoherently about dead people that "came out of the sandwiches". I figured maybe he said "sand" and I just heard it wrong, but I rewound this part several times and it's definitely "sandwiches". I also liked the part where one of the zombies, while chowing down on Microtits' leg, sticks a couple of his fingers right in her crotch. Pretty bold, but when you're a zombie I guess you have to get it any way you can.

Outpost

(2007)

Directed by Steve Barker

I swear, I'd love to know who okays some of these DVD covers. Seriously, look this one up and tell me that the guy on the front doesn't look like he's trying to come to terms with the fact that he just shit in his pants. If that's what he was going for – maybe because his character realizes that a bunch of Nazi zombies are creeping up behind him – then nice job, dude. Unfortunately, I think he was trying to look tough or something.

So, anyone who watches a lot of bad movies and/or the History Channel knows that the Nazis invented everything from flying saucers to the Pez dispenser, and the cat in this flick is trying to track down one of these inventions, a machine that trumps Einstein and makes Michio Katu look like he just fell off the turnip truck. Well, our boy does locate the gizmo in question, but there's an annoying by-product when you turn it on: Nazi ghosts. Or, to be more specific, the ghosts of invincible soldiers (read: zombies) that the Nazis created previously and then misplaced, somehow, I guess. I'm a little sketchy on the details, but who cares about details when you're watching a movie about (probably) the ghosts of Nazi zombies? I mean, holy shit. Nazi zombie ghosts. And notice how much more badass that is than if any of those words had been "vegetable". Anyway, the Nazi-zombie-ghosts ultimately kill everybody, which is to be expected. I mean, what else are they gonna do with those credentials? Raise bunnies? Start a book club? Teach children about the dangers of carbon monoxide? Use you head, man.

A pretty awesome flick.

Psychomania

(1973)

Directed by Don Sharp

People have longed to cheat death since at least the 1950's, and here it turns out some old bat had the secret stashed in her spare bedroom the whole time. Her son begs and begs until she finally lets him in on it, at which point he immediately commits suicide and comes back as an unkillable zombie biker, exploding out of his grave, bike and all, like the cover of a Meatloaf album. First order of business: filling up on petrol (this movie's British) and not paying. ("I'll teach you a lesson, you long-haired git," says the guy manning the petrol station. He's immediately owned.) Second order of business: selling the rest of his gang on the idea, which sounds like the Rx for awesome so it's a shame this movie just phones it in and squanders nearly every opportunity to be over the top. For example, during the funeral for one zombie biker the casket is opened and everyone's shocked because the body is gone, having revived and strolled off previously. But how much cooler would it have been if she had waited until the middle of the service, and then punched her way out of her own coffin, right in front of everybody? This flick does have its good points, like the bikers' weird fetish for running over baby carriages, or the scene where the camera slowly circles around this room full of cops - at first the cops are all alive, but when we come around again they're all dead. It's passage of time,

Rick. The bikers' suicides are pretty rock on too. One of them does this badass forward-facing Nestea plunge right off an overpass, and, in the single best part of the movie, a cop yells up to a biker on the seventh floor to come down and move his ride: "Okay," the dude says, and then, all casual-like, jumps out the window. There's not enough of this hilarious insanity though; most of the time they're just tooling down the highway in their queer-ass skull helmets. (I know the idea of a motorcycle helmet that looks like a skull sounds pretty boss, but trust me, they found a way to screw it up.) This flick isn't a total bust, but when all's said and done I don't think the Hell's Angels or the Pagans have anything to worry about. Or even the Punch-Drunk Banditos, assuming a motorcycle club with that name even exists. I sure hope it does.

The Quick and the Undead

(2006)

Directed by Gerald Nott

Okay, so the premise here, as I understand it, is that the zombie apocalypse occurred back in cowboy days, at which point culture, fashion, and technology came to a complete standstill and now in regular times there are still cowboys who hunt the zombies down for fun and profit. In theory, at least. In practice, all they really do is wander around the goddamned woods. And then there's the main guy, who's so fucking cool you won't be able to stand it, or him. Seriously, every time he posed in a doorway, looking all badass, I prayed that a small pioneer child would come running up and kick him right in the nards. We'll see how cool you look then, fuckdick, rolling around on the ground, crying like a bitch and cradling your swollen junk. And the whole conceit where they collect zombies' fingers for the bounty, could that make any more no sense whatsoever? Think about it - how do the authorities determine which are zombie fingers, and which are little-old-lady-who-was-way-easier-to-kill fingers? In the end everyone *finally* finds their way out of the woods (seriously, Hansel and Gretel didn't have this much trouble) and into an actual building, where they just wander around some more until the zombies finally get inside and kill them. Then they blatantly rip off the end of *Dawn of the Dead* and this boring piece of crap is finally over.

"Nott Entertainment" is the name of the company that produced this movie. I swear, sometimes these jokes just write themselves.

Raiders of the Living Dead

(1986)

Directed by Samuel M. Sherman

First off – and most importantly, given America's gradual transformation into a fully scam-based economy – this movie is a laudable example of truth in advertising. It really does feature a team of honest-to-fuck raiders of the living dead, consisting of the following:

- A kid who figures out how to build a laser pistol using an old laserdisc player (fun fact: this is why they stopped making those)
- Said kid's girlfriend (too young to fuck, but worth keeping an eye on)
- An old man with a target bow. Before the final raid on the living dead, he accessorizes with a fedora and a jaunty neckerchief.
- A douchey reporter who, after encountering the zombies *once,* immediately becomes a fugitive on the run. Just go home, you fucking drama queen. (Extra doucheiness factor: he likes the Three Stooges)
- A homely nurse
- A security guard who walks right off the job to become a raider of the living dead, and is immediately killed by zombies

And there's more: a gloriously bad theme song (get used to it, because you'll be hearing it a lot); a guy who gets out of his car and climbs lengthwise over a tanker truck to reach the cab when he could've simply driven up next to it; hilariously long reaction shots of people not reacting; the kid inadvertently killing a gerbil and terrorizing potential pedophiles with his homemade raygun; and, early on, a super-cute hostage chick who I totally want to bone.

Honestly, I don't see how anyone could hate this movie.

Raw Force

(1982)

Directed by Edward Murphy

Three kung fu aces are on vacation when their boat sinks during a pirate attack. Making their way to shore, they find themselves on an island run by evil monks who don't take kindly to, well, anyone, so they raise a gaggle of kung fu zombies from the grave and everybody fights. As you can see, this is already one of the best movies ever made, but, astoundingly, it gets *better,* because, finally, this is the movie we've all been waiting for: the movie that has, literally, *everything.* There's scads of naked chicks, a bar brawl, a guy's face shoved into the toilet, slavery (white and regular), gunplay, cannibals, piranhas, and, of course, oodles of gore. Truth be told, *Raw Force* is the greatest anything that has ever been created, ever, with the possible exception of boobs but, as noted, it does have those in it. If you haven't seen this movie then you might as well be a 41-year-old virgin, or the only guy in your sewing circle who's never even tasted booze. I urge you, if you do nothing else with your life, if you never achieve, obtain, or create *anything* of any value whatsoever, at least, *at least,* see this movie. And then you can go back to being Joey Greco with your head held at least a little higher.

Redneck Zombies

(1987)

Directed by Pericles Lewnes

The best thing about our last flick (besides everything, I mean) is that you can win bar bets by insisting that Eddie Murphy once wrote and directed a kung fu zombie movie. The best thing about this flick, on the other hand, is nothing. In fact, this universally despised *Hee Haw*/zombie mash-up is one of the movies that started the whole trend of being bad on purpose, as if this somehow makes the director's mother any less of a whore. Speaking of *Hee Haw* and zombies, I think this would have been a good bit:

STUDIO AUDIENCE: *"Hey Grandpa, what's for supper?"*

GRANDPA JONES: "Me! *Oh God no!!!!*" [Is eaten by zombies.]

ROY CLARK: "I always wondered when those guys would *meat.*"

STUDIO AUDIENCE: [Groans]

S0 anyway, the trouble starts – well, for us, it's starts the instant this movie begins, because it sucks ass – but the in-story trouble starts when this fat redneck ganks a barrel of radioactive chemical warfare waste from the army guy who's transporting it. Of course the local slackjaws decide to use the barrel as a still (because that's the stupidest thing that could possibly happen), and pretty soon it's a zombie hick-pocalypse, much to the chagrin of our heroes: two black people and their fattie-loving, honky friends (there's a twist, right?) who are camping nearby. Gory but worthless, this movie is now available as a "Special Edition", which proves, conclusively, that everyone on Earth is a complete asshole.

Remains

(2011)

Directed by Colin Theys

Just for the record, the actual on-screen title of this movie is **Steve Niles' Remains**. I'm not sure if this is because someone thought that this Steve Niles joker had some sort of name recognition (wrong) or because he's especially impressed with himself, but either way I'm not typing a bunch of extra letters just to stoke his out-of-control ego. Trust me people, if you don't want to look like a complete tool, *never* tack your name onto the title of something you've created. That's Mr. Satanism's First Rule of Titles.

Alright, so there's zombies, and this time the people they want to eat are holed up in a casino, which isn't such a bad place to be because those places are fucking *stocked*. They'll die of blood alcohol poisoning long before the zombies get in. (Actually, I'm told that dying of blood alcohol poisoning is a pretty painful way to go. There's always a catch.) I guess our heroes miss daylight and easily-located clocks though, because they decide to escape, and in this they do have one distinct advantage: these zombies actually go to sleep when it gets dark! The solution is almost childishly simple: be like those Polish astronauts who wanted to land on the sun, and leave at night. They don't do that though. Instead, they go out of their way to draw the attention of some Dickhead Zombie Movie Military Guys™, who proceed to ruin everything. (You may remember this development from every zombie movie ever made, but it's worth pointing out that it's inclusion is especially lazy and uninspired here.) The part where two people learn that it's impossible to escape from a locked parking garage using standard movie methods (driving through the gate; shooting the security keypad) is kinda funny, but other than that this flick is complete garbage. The months-later commercial for the Blu-ray, done in the style of the Nastyass Honey Badger ("Think zombies care? They don't give a shit.") was infinitely more entertaining. Maybe you should learn a few things from it, Steve Niles.

The Return of the Living Dead (Workprint)

(1985)

Directed by Dan O'Bannon

Return of the Living Dead is one of the best movies ever made, so when I had the opportunity to see this illegal bootleg version containing stuff they ultimately cut out I couldn't pass it up. I'll do anything if I know it's illegal. If you never get a chance to see it though, rest assured you're not missing much; there's no deleted scene where the two hot-ass punk chicks dyke out or anything. Everything just takes a little longer, and even when there is something new it's generally people sitting around doing nothing or talking about buying sodas. The only interesting parts are a slightly different ending (all the contaminated zombie dirt ends up in a rail yard in South Dakota), the warehouse guy calls the black dude a "black bastard" instead of "dick brain" (probably changed so he wouldn't seem racist), the main punk calls the one chick "chocolate face" instead of "ball-buster" (probably changed because calling a white person "chocolate face" makes no goddamned sense whatsoever), and exhibitionist punkette "Trash" strips to a Vanity 6 song instead of SSQ. I'm sure if George Lucas or Steven Spielberg had made this movie they would've gone and put all this stuff back in (plus added a bunch of cartoon zombies and probably replaced Trash's tits with walkie-talkies) but frankly it's all pretty unnecessary. I did like this excised line though:

EMBALMER/NAZI WAR CRIMINAL GUY: "Don't you worry about Freddie and Frank. See, they've gone to Heaven. Those things, they're just dead bodies that want to eat our brains."

I think that 's gonna be my new ring tone.

Return of the Living Dead: Necropolis

(2005)

Directed by Ellory Elkayem

The military's zombie reanimating gas, seen in all previous "Return of the Living Dead" movies (this is Part 4), is now firmly in the hands of the private sector, and one facility is already creating their very own zombies, which are nourished on the fakest-looking rubber brains you've ever seen, even if your job happens to be processing returns at the worst rubber brain manufacturing plant in the entire fucking world. Apparently they're a little short on funds though, because they're reduced to kidnapping a teenager from the hospital for additional experimentation, and right in front of their high school intern yet, prompting her to round up the gang and do what teenagers always do in situations like this: complain how it totally sucks and that no one understands them. Ha ha! Actually, they raid the place on motorbikes. Of course they end up freeing all the zombies, so the guy in charge, thoroughly pissed, sics some *zombie Borg* on them. (I like how the government couldn't achieve jack shit with this zombie gas over the course of three movies, but as soon as it hits the private sector people are immediately producing zombie Borg. Capitalism works. Fuck you, Micheal Moore.) Unfortunately, these *Return of the Living Dead* zombies are ridiculously pussified when compared to previous incarnations, easily taken out with gunfire or even a punch to the face. Worse yet, the intern chick, who's a real cutie, never gets naked! This is the same bullshit they pulled in Part 2: the hot redhead in that installment didn't get naked either. I think the best way to determine which of these sequels you'll hate the most is to decide which of the two actresses in question (Jana Kramer or Suzanne Snyder) you'll be more disappointed by when she doesn't show us her tits. Me, I'm a gentleman, so I'm gonna call it a draw. Ladies, I want to see *both* your tits. I mean, from the both of you. I mean... damn it... What I mean is, I want *both* of you to show me *both* your tits. All right then.

Return of the Living Dead: Rave to the Grave

(2005)

Directed by Ellory Elkayem

The only reason this sequel got the green light is because it wouldn't be practical to travel around the world and kick every single person who liked the other *Return of the Living Dead* movies in the balls individually. The main kid from the previous sequel returns as the same character, but apparently he has teen Alzheimer's or something because he doesn't seem to remember a thing about it, including what zombies even are. When some additional zombie reanimatrix turns up his pinhead, raver friends use it to get high, with the expected results, but first it makes everyone's head jerk wildly around at super speed, a visual effect moviemakers had a *raging* hard-on for at the time, despite the fact that it looks inexcusably fake and gay. (Also note that this is the stupidest plot that anyone has ever come up with for a movie, ever.) There are a few good elements – a chick is bitten on the ass; zombies are attacking a car full of hippies when a third party blows the car up with a rocket launcher, neatly eliminating both problems; and there are some nice tits – but these are completely overshadowed by the endless, rampant stupidity, like the moronic scene where a zombie is decapitated with a *guitar* (maybe if it had been some

Civil War zombie that was all desiccated and shit, but this one's pretty fresh). Trust me, tits aside this movie is wasteland of shit. It should be avoided like a unstable fat chick with the clap.

By the way, here's a newsflash: if you look at the calendar and it says "2005", it might be a little late to make a movie about rave, grandpa. Try reading a magazine or something so you have at least some idea what the fuck is going on.

Revenge of the Zombies

(1943)

Directed by Steve Sekely

This broad dies under mysterious circumstances, so her brother shows up, sidekick in tow, to look into it. The sidekick is a black guy whose racist-stereotype schtick would put Bernie Mac to shame: at the very beginning, for example, he suddenly breaks out in this little song and dance, in a stranger's driveway, for absolutely no reason. He's a singin', dancin' jigaboo! Sorry, I mean "differently-abled". Anyway, it turns out the dead woman's husband is a mad scientist who's secretly making zombies for the Nazis. You'd think he'd cool it for a while, what with his brother-in-law nosing around and all, but nope – he's got corpses overtly roaming all over the grounds, including his zombified wife, whose mysterious death, you may recall, is what aroused all this suspicion in the first place. Not exactly a master of subtlety, our mad doctor, not that it matters since he's ultimately betrayed by his secretary, his servants, *and* the zombies, *plus* it turns out that his Nazi contact is really an undercover agent for the United States! Frankly, I felt kind of sorry for the guy. What a loser.

Revolt of the Zombies

(1936)

Directed by Victor Halperin

Nobody believes this Cambodian when he says he can whip up some zombies to help fight the Great World War (AKA World War Part 1), but when he goes and proves it they put him in jail! You can't win for losing. Later they decide to send an expedition to Cambodia to locate and suppress their zombie-making process, since it could be quite dangerous if it fell into the wrong hands and besides their beliefs and culture are stupid anyway. Unfortunately, the guy who finally tracks the secret down is both evil and an utter tool: he creates a entire army of zombies, but can't think of anything better for them to do than help him strong-arm some ugly broad into marrying him! Then he sets them all free just because this old wheelchair dude tells him he's being a jerk! How wishy-washy can you get? Worst of all, the zombies only claim a single victim: a dickhead who tries to obtain the zombie formula from the main guy using flattery ("You are a clod. I, a man of imagination."). It's probably the weakest zombie movie ever made, and the part where our main guy trails some joker through the swamp features the phoniest-looking shots of people walking I've ever laid eyes on. Honestly, this is beyond fucking pathetic. How do you screw up a scene of people *walking?*

Rise of the Zombies

(2012)

Directed by Nick Lyon

Let's see, military types and scientists, holed up in a secure location, arguing about how to deal with the zombie apocalypse. Where have I seen this setup before? Oh yeah, and that movie sucked. Fortunately, *these* unlikeable assholes are ousted from their hidey-hole almost immediately, after which they break off into two groups. The first group, led by Machete, is almost entirely wiped out by one disturbingly sexy, oh-so-flexible zombie chick, although in their defense she probably would've gotten me too, and you don't want to know what I'd be trying to do when she did. The second group, led by this decrepit ol' lady, fares somewhat better - they actually manage to locate French Stewart who, it seems, has developed a vaccine for the zombie virus, giving us all hope for a zombie-free future. (A similar promise was made if *World War Z* tanked at the box office.) Meanwhile, Geordi La Forge, ever the idiot, studies the phenomenon by cutting a chunk out of his own arm, feeding it to his zombie daughter, and then standing so close while she eats it that she manages to bite him anyway. Haven't you ever owned a dog, Geordi? *Don't crowd them while they're eating.* There are some good/creepy scenes (a zombie attack on a raft, zombies climbing the Golden Gate Bridge), and, in a standout bit of tastelessness, an impromptu c-section is performed on a pregnant chick after she's bitten by a zombie, only to have the baby zombify anyway via the umbilical cord, at which point someone stomps it to death. Plus: suicide by grenade and bus crash; the fat guy from *My Name is Earl* loses an arm; and we learn that zombies are especially susceptible to Tasers, and are afraid of dogs. Huh. Just like black people.

Slightly-above-average zombie shenanigans.

The Roost

(2005)

Directed by Ti West

I wouldn't say killer bat movies are a dime a dozen, but they're definitely overvalued, so it's nice to see this one employ some gimmicks to make it stand out from the rest of the colony. (That's what you call a flock of bats: a *colony*. See, this book is educational as well as tasteless.) Their first gimmick is that they made *The Roost* look just like a sub-par 1970's horror movie, right down to having a goofy *Scream Theatre* style intro, like it's playing on some local TV station circa 1980. This would be beyond fucking cool, if they didn't fuck the whole thing up. First off, back in the 1970's moviemakers used a little something called a "tripod". They didn't just wave the camera around like a drunken sailor on whore leave. And second, for some unfathomable reason the main hottie is carrying around a 2000's-era **cell phone**. *People in the 1970's didn't have modern cell phones, you goddamned idiots.* Seriously, I hate dilholes who think that the world and everything in it popped into existence the day they were born and will end the day I finally get fed up with their self-centered bullshit and murder them. Rest assured, there was a whole range of human experience that occurred before you came along, choad breath, and, just so you know, surprisingly little of it involved looking at Internet porn in the dark while crying. Fortunately, this movie's second gimmick is much more effectively realized: it seems that everyone these particular bats bite turns into a bona fide zombie! (As opposed to a fraudulent zombie, obviously.) This strongly implies that the bats are zombies themselves, and you really can't go wrong with a concept like "zombie bats". It's a fun, wild idea that they do almost nothing with - not unlike (thus keeping with the premise) your typical sub-par 1970's horror movie. So in the end this flick is alright, although the whole cell phone thing still irks me to no end. Seriously, the fact that the characters have a cell phone handy doesn't even play into the story, so why bother including it at all? Stupid assholes.

Seven Mummies

(2006)

Directed by Nick Quested

Some crooks manage to escape from a prison van after it flips over, and while we don't actually see how this accident comes about I'm going to assume that it involves Coors, or possibly Coors Light. The crooks make a beeline for Mexico, but along the way they meet this crazy Indian (casino, not 7-11) who says that there's gold in them thar hills, by which I mean that thar desert. Since he has no proof whatsoever they assume it must be true, so they go looking for the gold and end up... Let's see, how can I explain this? If *From Dusk Till Dawn* (1996) was a verb, that's what happens to them. Unlike *From Dusk Till Dawn*, however, this movie is a complete fucking ripoff, because the mummies touted by the title don't even show up until the last fifteen minutes! Seriously, when I watch a movie called "Seven Mummies" I expect *seven times* more mummy than I'd get from a regular movie, not four times less. And there's issues with the nudity, too: one hooker they encounter pops out a set so fake and disgusting that I damn near puked, but the two genuinely hot chicks on deck never show us a thing. So while this flick does, technically, have mummies and tits in it, realistically it's like saying an event was catered because someone threw a 3 Musketeers bar through the window. That sneaky "read the fine print" shit might fool a ninth-rate movie critic like Leonard Maltin, but they're not putting one over on Mr. Satanism. *Seven Mummies* can smoke my fucking pole. And so can you, Maltin. Two-and-a-half stars for *Alien* (1979)? You're such a know-nothing fuckhole.

Severed

(2005)

Directed by Carl Bessai

Hippies tend to dislike huge, environmentally-unconscious corporations, and the people who run huge, environmentally-unconscious corporations tend to dislike hippies. Me, I hate 'em both, so I found it really hard to root for anyone in this movie besides the zombies. And while adding lumberjacks to the mix held some promise, given their access to extremely powerful saws (suck it, trees), nothing really comes of this: *Severed* is lazily content to fall into the same old zombie movie rut, right down to including lumberjack stand-ins for your stock Dickhead Zombie Movie Military Guys™. And I hate to be nit-picky (Ha ha! No I don't.), but this movie's timeline is seriously confused: as a result of zombie terror, no one has heard from this lumber camp long enough for there to be legitimate concern at the corporate level, but when the main guy shows up to investigate it's like the zombie outbreak just began a few minutes ago. I mean, how else could the whale-hugging protestor who's been chained to a tree still be completely unharmed? (Incidentally, it does turn out that being chained to a tree is a bad position to be in during a crisis situation.) We never get a good look at the zombies because the cameraman has a seizure every time they appear (if you're that afraid of zombies, maybe you shouldn't have taken a gig on a zombie movie, pussy), but they do shoot a guy who won't stop sounding off about Jesus and, in the tradition of Julia Hill, the main envirochick is super hot, so it's not the worst zombie movie ever made. It could've been a helluva lot better though.

Heh. "Root" for anyone.

6teen: "Dude of the Living Dead"

(2005)

Directed by Karen Lessmann and Gary Hurst

Not so long ago, at least as old people reckon shit, *Dawn of the Dead* (1978) was understood to be one of the goriest, most repulsive movies around. Now it's fodder for a Canadian children's cartoon about teenagers who work at the mall. Seriously, if the zombie apocalypse gets any more diluted, undead fuckers will be allowed to vote. As a general rule, cartoons about teenagers appeal primarily to preteens (the only demographic that actually finds teenagers cool), and this show is no exception, what with its juvenile, gross-out jokes about popping zits and puking in a chick's mouth. This episode does feature more severed limbs than you'd normally see in a kids' show, but the way their little zombie mini-pocalypse plays out is pretty obvious, right up to the *of-course*-it-was-all-a-dream cop-out ending. Frankly, the biggest surprise is that they've included one main character sporting an "88" on his t-shirt (fucking racist), and another one who's a blatant pothead. Apparently Canadians are a lot less uptight about their kids dabbling in neo-Nazism and dope than we are.

Subject Two

(2006)

Directed by Philip Chidel

Wow, a boring, pretentious version of *Re-Animator* (1985). That's on *my* list too, right above a nuclear North Korea, and just below banning boobs. The subject in question doesn't like it much either, because in this movie being re-animated hurts like hell, prompting the mad doctor who's throwing this party to deaden his nerves, making him incapable of feeling anything. You know, like a woman. Ha ha! The nerve-deadening process works, but obviously jerking off will never be the same so our zombified subject decides that he wants to die for real, leading, predictably, to endless helpings of grief for everyone involved. (Okay, fine, they never single out jerking off as the impetus, but it makes sense to me.) Unexpected side effects, uncooperative test subjects... as you can see, this whole experiment has been a clusterfuck from day one. But I guess that's what makes mad scientists mad - they never know when to throw in the towel and just coast on the tenure. And it would've been nice if they'd told us – you know, the audience – exactly how this looney sawbones was bringing people back to life in the first place. Heavy doses of electricity? A magical elixir? Postmortem romp with Misty Mundae? I realize the answer would be pseudo-scientific gobbledygook; I'm not asking for a step-by-step here. Just throw us a bone, huh? After all, with no mad science there's not much in this mad scientist movie to hold your attention, unless you enjoy stupid mistakes, like when the doctor is balls-deep in a body and then touches his eyes and/or nose without washing his hands. Oh, wait, there is the gratuitous blonde... she's so adorable! Can someone please explain why we never see her tits? You sure as hell don't hire someone as cute as her for her acting ability, even if she has some.

So, to sum things up: this is a mad scientist movie with no science, that's only entertaining when it's stupid, and it features a hot blonde who doesn't get naked. I don't care how many times you brought this flick back to life, it would still suck.

Sugar Hill

(1974)

Directed by Paul Maslansky

"Sugar Hill" is the actual name of the main character in this movie, and she's not even a stripper! What would she do if she ever did become a stripper, and needed a stripper name? She'd have to call herself "Jenny Smith" or something. Anyway, Sugar is royally pissed when some hoods dis her man by kicking him to death in the parking lot, though if you ask me he totally had it coming what with that Sparkle Tags suit he was sporting. Seriously, even for a 1970's black person, it's completely ridiculous. Sugar calls on Baron Samedi (you know, from *Live and Let Die*), but he refuses to accept her soul in exchange for revenge. He prefers pussy! He likes the cut of her jib though, so he loans her some freaky-ass, silver-eyed, machete-toting zombies to sic on the bad guys. With his boys suddenly dropping left and right, the main bad guy sends his number two to get the 411 by leaning on "every chippie, every client, every squeaker", but he doesn't grok what's really going down until it's entirely too late. (Neither does the cop who's on the case, but seeing as he's a brother and has to go to some cracker to learn about the voodoo, this isn't exactly surprising.) Since these are voodoo zombies, not flesh-eating zombies, it's all fairly tame by your typical zombie movie standards, but we still get a catfight, a decapitation, man-eating pigs, a rampaging chicken foot, a zombie massage with an unhappy ending, and plenty more hoodoo wanna voodoo insanity. If that's not enough for you, I dunno, go pull the wings off some flies or something.

Survival of the Dead

(2009)

Directed by George A. Romero

I never thought I'd say this, but George Romero can suck my fucking dick. Sure, his original *Dawn of the Dead* is one of the finest motion pictures ever made (second only to *Raw Force*, and possibly *Hannah Montana: The Movie*), but his talent for making zombie movies has improved with age like a fine wine stored too close to the furnace, and he **just won't stop**. *Day of the Dead, Land of the Dead, Diary of the Dead*... they all suck shit. And you can add this one, which is Part 6, to his inauspicious oeuvre ("oeuvre" is French for "eggs"). For real, why do people even bother with these stale turds when you can watch *The Walking Dead* on AMC for free? Assuming you're stealing your cable of course, which, naturally, I am.

Let's see, do I even want to take the time to list everything that's wrong with this flick? The story is dumb; most of the "good guys" are annoying dicks; everyone acts like some 12-year-old's idea of a badass, lighting their cigarettes off burning zombies and shit (when the people in *Dawn of the Dead* behaved like this it inevitably backfired on them, which was far more realistic and entertaining); some of the kills are beyond stupid (Trust me, if you shoot a fire extinguisher into someone's mouth their eyes don't pop out of their sockets in a gory/comical fashion. They just have to get their stomach pumped and then break up with you.); and how many "I was actually aiming for the zombie sneaking up behind you" fake-outs does one movie need? Oh, and let's not forget the big "twist" where it turns out that the chick we thought was dead ~~has~~ had a *twin sister*. Are you FUCKING kidding me? This movie needs to pay its bar tab and leave *immediately* before I kick its fucking ass. "It's over," says the chick who's really her twin sister at the end. We should be so lucky, bitch - rumor has it that ol' George has at least two more zombie movies on the drawing board. I just hope that by the time he gets financing, one of us is dead.

Swamp Zombies!!!

(2005)

Directed by Len Kabasinski

There's nothing like a surprise federal inspection to panic a mad doctor into dumping his experimental zombies in the nearest swamp. Also visiting the swamp: some annoying college students – including three notably hot chicks (okay, fine, one of them does have the moon face going on, but I'd still hit it) – plus assorted anglers, park rangers, sexy-ass bikini babes, and, eventually, cops, many of whom will end up as lunch for our zombies. This flick is way too long (nearly two hours); it could've been a lot gorier (more zombies are taken out via impromptu kung fu than head shots); shit is poorly choreographed (the fight scenes are still better than the ones in *Corpses are Forever* though); their isolated attempts at humor fall flatter than Jessica's chest; the camerawork, editing, and acting are all sub-par (the acting being especially atrocious); and the music is unforgivably gay (I'm looking at you, "Criminally Insane"). That said, it's never boring, and, with the exception of one pair of utterly repugnant fakes, there are lots of high-quality tits. This isn't a good movie by any commonly accepted definition of the term, but even after it's over it's *still* introducing new characters who show us their tits, and for that, it's earned my respect. Okay, maybe "respect" isn't the right word, but I sure would like to meet some of their actresses.

Terror-Creatures from the Grave

(1965)

Directed by Ralph Zucker

A lawyer arrives at this creepy old villa to prepare some cat's will, only to learn that the guy died a *year* ago. You really need to do something about that backlog, dipshit. And now there's an owl caught in his car engine (okay, what?), so he's stuck there. With nothing better to do he decides to throw some game at this chick who happens to be staying at the villa, even though she's obviously nuts, constantly flipping out and insisting that she sees dead people. But she is cute, and he is a guy, so needless to say that doesn't slow him down too much. And it turns out she's not just whistling "Dixie" - this dead guy really has returned from the grave to seek revenge on the dude who wasted him, plus five other jokers who got a big laugh out of it because really, how rude. One of the clowns the dead guy is gunning for is in a wheelchair now, and, rather than let the zombie get him, he braces a sword in a cabinet door, blade out, and just wheels himself right into it. (This works surprising well. If you're in a wheelchair and are thinking about killing yourself – you know, because you can't walk and shit – you might want to write that one down.) It's a pretty gruesome bit for 1965, and some of wheelchair guy's guts even leak out, clinching this as the best part of the movie, especially since none of the chicks get naked. In the end, several zombies carrying the plague pop out of the ground to help the main zombie out; I assume these are the "terror-creatures from the grave" we've been promised, but all we ever see are their shadows! How unbelievably weak is that??? You can't call your movie "Terror-Creatures from the Grave" and then skimp on the goddamned terror-creatures! I don't know what goes through peoples' heads sometimes. This movie sucks.

Toxic Zombies

(1980)

Directed by Charles McCrann

Toxic Zombies begins with a couple of federal agents blowing away a chick in the woods – apparently, they mistook her for a hippie – prompting two actual hippies to make short work of them in turn. Why all the negativity? Well, it seems the hippies are babysitting two million dollars worth of dope they've got growing nearby, and the Federal Drug Intelligence Agency (or whoever) wants to destroy it. In pursuit of this, they dust the whole damn area with a dangerous new defoliant that turns everyone into semi-sophisticated flesh-eating zombies that are smart enough to use weapons and make fire, but not smart enough to simply order in some steak tartare. There's one set of solid tits, a reasonable amount of gore, a retard who is *not* letting go of his plush rhinoceros, some hilariously hateful domestic squabbling ("Gimme that phone ya goddamned bitch!"), a hot secretary, some government treachery, a woman who can't get a truck to start so turns everything else (wipers, lights) on instead, a truly bizarre monologue about a lumber accident, and tons of hilarious dialogue, including a line about fungus later borrowed, inexplicably, by the cult classic *The Carrier* (1988). Oh, and I like how the movie opens with a shot of the people who instigate the horror driving towards us, and closes on the guy who vanquished it driving away at the opposite angle. It's fucking artistic, man. Or, more likely, pure coincidence. All-in-all a pretty good, if mostly forgotten, classic-era zombie flick.

28 Days Later

(2002)

Directed by Danny Boyle

Look, I like bunnies and unicorns as much as the next guy, but I am so tired of hearing about animal rights. I get all my meals from fast food restaurants anyway, so who needs animals? In this flick, the animal rights contingent liberates some zombie monkeys, and you can imagine where that leads: 28 days later our main guy (I think he's one of the GEICO cavemen) wakes up in the hospital to a full-on zombie jamboree. At first he can't find anybody though, so what does he do? He goes to church! If you think you missed the Rapture, it's a little late now, assbrains. When he finally does catch up he joins some fellow survivors (including a little chickie who's too young to be so hot but OMG she just is) and they head for the hills, pausing along the way only to rip off every single scene from *Dawn of the Dead* (the buying groceries scene; the stopping for gas, poking around an empty building, and being forced to kill a small child scene). Eventually our heroes hook up with some soldiers, who, in a development that will come as a surprise to absolutely no one, turn out to be Dickhead Zombie Movie Military Guys™. Their leader is pretty eager to get on with the treachery and rape, but our main guy manages to free the zombie they keep chained in the backyard and it fucks most of them up. When are the people in these movies gonna learn not to keep zombies as pets? And why is it that no amount of military training can prevent guys from being duped by a hot chick? If I ran the military, I would cover that on day one. Also I'd take back Cuba. This movie is gory enough, but there aren't any tits, unless you count one pair of zombie tits, and I don't. (Although I might make an exception for that *Rise of the Zombies* chick I mentioned previously.) They do show the main guy naked, though - twice! And they *repeatedly* find excuses to show him with his shirt off. I don't care what you do in the privacy of your own home, Danny Boyle (or in public for that matter), but don't use your zombie movie to push your gay agenda on me. Save it for some artsy-fartsy vampire flick.

2 Hours

(2012)

Directed by Michael Ballif

Okay, who ordered yet another redundant, pointless zombie short? Seriously, who was it? Was it you? I'm talking to you, in the back, the one sporting the Deicide shirt and drinking Miller Ultra. It *was* you, wasn't it? You stupid asshole. The one saving grace here, as we watch yet another random dink wander around after the zombie armageddon, self-consciously narrating his woes and tribulations to a completely uncaring audience (that would be us), is that this stinker actually clocks in at under thirty minutes, not the two hours the title suggests. If nothing else, that does make it only 25% as painful as it could have been. It's still an endurance test though, especially during the endless, laughably "deep" final speech our annoying "hero" gives, which feels like it's ended a good eight times before it actually does. Seriously, folks, this one is *painful,* and I wouldn't recommended it to anyone I liked, or whose pants I was trying to get into, or most strangers. I would recommend it to my worst enemy though. Because why wouldn't I? Seriously, I hate it when hyperbolic people say that they wouldn't do some unpleasant thing to their worst enemy. Of course you fucking would. Who are you trying to kid?

Valley of the Zombies

(1946)

Directed by Philip Ford

This cat shows up at a hospital, railing that he was unfairly committed to the nuthouse. Oh, and he'd also like some human blood, to go. Okay, so he's not too self-aware, but it's hard to hold this against the guy once we learn that he's dead! Yup, thanks to an elixir he picked up in the Valley of the Zombies (no overnight camping, all dogs must be on leash), he's the walking, talking (lots of talking) dead. The catch? He needs blood to "counteract the effect". That's right, he's a bona fide zom– er, vampire. Who doesn't know what "counteract" means. Once word gets out you'd think everybody would hightail it to this Valley of the Zombies for Act 2, but nope. They do drive across town though, where they break into a mausoleum and a spooky old mansion. Along the way everyone makes Bob Hope-style wisecracks ("We're number one on their hate parade.") and drops alliteration like "this peculiar party that has a passion for pickling", but it's all surprisingly tolerable, thanks to a high body count and a main chick who's totally useless but decidedly fuckable. So I guess she isn't *totally* useless after all, at least until she tries to cook you a post-coital pot pie, accidentally burns the whole house down, and is subsequently eaten by a zombie cow. Trust me, with this bitch, it could happen.

Vampires vs. Zombies

(2004)

Directed by Vince D'Amato

It's a pretty good bet that when somebody comes up with an idea as sick as "Vampires vs. Zombies" they're gonna find some way to screw it up, but this time they didn't and holy *shit* is this movie the tits. This guy and his white-hot daughter (who's rocking the sexiest legs of all time, and that's official because I am officially in charge of deciding this) are on the run during yet another zombie holocaust when they cross paths with a second hottie who just happens to be a lesbian vampire. First chance she gets, our *nosferati lesbisch* dykes it up with the daughter and puts the bite on one of her impressive thighs, after which our story deteriorates into a free-for-all in which the dad wants to kill the vampire, the zombies want to kill and eat the humans, and the vampire just wants to eat the daughter's pussy. In addition to the aforementioned legs and lesbo action we've got blood spewing everywhere, zombies ripping peoples' guts out, one chick puts her fist through a zombie's head, both main hotties show off their racks, and towards the end they even trot out some zombified Catholic schoolgirls! Needless to say, this movie doesn't just rule, it rules with an iron fucking fist. You know the Academy Awards are fixed if it didn't win *something*.

Vengeance of the Zombies

(1973)

Directed by Leon Klimovsky

Two grave robbers are sacking a mausoleum when this voodoo priest shows up and resurrects their mark as a zombie that immediately kills them. The zombie's cousin (I think) attends a séance, then braves a house that's supposedly under a curse so she can visit the resident guru. Suddenly the cousin is dragged into a room where a demon, a hot chick covered with gold paint, and several zombies stab her and catch some of her blood in a cup. The demon drinks her blood, but before anything else can happen it turns out this scene is all a dream. (Note: weak.) Shortly thereafter, a mime stabs a couple who are getting it on down at the cold meat plant, and later more zombies come to life in the morgue. There's tits, gore, a decapitation, a rake fight, zombie-on-cop violence, and a hot blonde is shot. Oh, and crazy jazz music plays whenever anything evil goes down. Your guess is as good as mine, but I think one chick sums it up best when she asks "What is happening here? What's it all about?"

The Video Dead

(1987)

Directed by Robert Scott

This drunk receives an all-expense-paid television set, with no idea who sent it to him. "I don't even watch TV," he says. Is that a fact? Then why doesn't he immediately hock it for more booze? Sounds like someone didn't think this plot through very carefully. Anyway, as you'd imagine, it's a scam: the TV is cursed, and that night several zombies crawl out of the evil idiot box and do the drunk in. And speaking of magical boxes, you should see the blonde who shows up a little later. *So* lickable. The pooch she's dog-sitting is immediately killed by the renegade zombies (still lurking in the nearby woods), and soon other, more atypical zombies appear, including one that takes the form of a trashy, topless chick. (Too bad she turns out to be a total tease. Fucking zombies.) This flick isn't outrageously gory, but it's solid enough, with decent zombie makeup; some blood; a then-zombie that could pass for now-David Bowie; and the aforementioned blonde looking deliriously fine in a white skirt/pink sweater ensemble. I have to say, as much as I love my goth chicks, punk rock bitches, and ninja assassin babes, there's nothing like a girl sporting a pink and/or white, sweater/skirt combo. It's why, twenty years later, I still have intricate sexual fantasies starring Sydney and Nicole.

P.S. If you're reading this, Sydney, hit me up. Not you, Nicole.

Voodoo Black Exorcist

(1974)

Directed by M. Caño

Naming your movie by cherry-picking words from the titles of other flicks that were popular at the time is bad enough, but at least have the sense to put them in the right order. "Voodoo Black" should be a color in the jumbo-sized box of Crayola crayons though, don't you think? I'll bet black people would love that. Jesse Jackson would probably organize another "Ban the Crayon" protest. Remember the first one, back in 1990? Seriously, this was a real thing: a bunch of people got mad because Crayola replaced some of the colors, so they wanted to boycott the company until they brought back "burnt umber" and "orange-blue" or whichever ones it was. This is another reason why, whenever I meet someone nostalgic about the 1990's, I immediately punch them in the throat.

So anyway, our black exorcist voodoo is highly irritated when they decapitate his woman, bury him alive, and then dig him up a thousand years later and take him on a tacky cruise, so he pops out of his coffin, kills a pussycat, decapitates a guy, and leaves the severed head in this chick's cabin. Later some clown tries to steal his ring, so the exorcist black voodoo backhands this fool, stabs him in the neck, and makes him his voodoo slave. Even when he disembarks, he uses his limited time on shore to run someone over with a steamroller and engage in a ridiculous tussle with a fire hose. The funniest part though is when he's slapping around this bitch with enormous tits, because you can clearly see the camera crew reflected in her makeup mirror! Professionalism, thy name is not *Voodoo Black Exorcist*. In the end the cops completely immolate the voodoo exorcist black with a flamethrower, even though he happens to be carrying off the main chick at the time! They just write her off as collateral damage! Ha ha! That's fucking great. This movie's still retarded though.

Waking Eloise

(2010)

Directed by Bobby Marinelli

Jesus H. Legba, there are so many romantic zombie comedies (rom-zom-coms) coming out these days that they might as well have their own, dedicated section in that abandoned building where the Blockbuster used to be. In this one, a pussy-whipped dork's girlfriend dies after being hit by lightning from a clear, blue sky, leading me to believe that she was intentionally murdered by God. Quickly tiring of masturbating to Internet porn, crying, and doing both of these things simultaneously, he consults a voodoo houngan dude (say it three times really fast) and brings her back, first as a zombie, and then, after employing some additional magic, as her formerly lovely self. Then he changes his mind and abandons her to die horribly (again) so he can take up with some broad he met a few hours ago. It's obvious we're supposed to applaud this ruthless decision because the revived girlfriend is bitchy and shallow, but truth be told she doesn't seem all *that* bad, and really, if you're gonna bring your girlfriend back to life and then act all wishy-washy about it while macking on other chicks, can you blame her for being a little pissed off? I mean seriously, what a fucking weasel.

Totally predictable and a huge waste of time. The girlfriend is pretty hot though.

When Good Ghouls Go Bad

(2001)

Directed by Patrick Read Johnson

Halloween is banned in Walker Falls because some goth kid laid down a curse back in the 1980's, and even though there's no proof whatsoever that this curse is legit people won't light so much as a single jack o' lantern for fear that he'll return and... I dunno, make them listen to Christian Death or something. One day though this businesscat decides to organize a big Halloween whatsit to impress some investors, and suddenly a huge mountain of pumpkins appears in the middle of town and one of them falls right on Doc Brown and kills him. Now, if this were a story in a Charlton comic book that would be the nonsensical "twist" ending that would leave us wishing we'd used our sixty cents to buy a box of Cherry Chans (if only for the hilarious, racist packaging), but in this case the raving stupidity has only begun. First, Doc Brown returns from the grave, on an ill-defined mission to save some or all of the following:

- Halloween
- His family's chocolate factory
- The local economy
- His grandson's relationship with his father
- The grandson's chances to get laid

Then a dismembered hand that's controlled by fireflies starts making the rounds, a G-rated zombie invasion occurs, and finally the goth kid reappears and exposes the most far-fetched cover-up in film history, and I'm including all previous and future *X-Files* movies when I say this. None of it makes any goddamned sense, especially the title. Who, in all of this, is the "good ghoul gone bad"? Having a stupid pun as the title of your movie is bad enough, but if you absolutely must go that route at least come up with one that applies to the story, you half-baked morons. Watching this miserable disaster is like going trick-or-treating and getting nothing but toothbrushes. With razor blades in them.

Where's My Mummy?

(2005)

Directed by Joe Sichta

More like, where's your fucking head? No, please specify *whose* ass. Seriously, how hard is it to make a Scooby-Doo movie? Mix one part Shaggy and Scooby running away from monsters, two parts Daphne looking fine, a couple of sly jokes for the grown-ups (Daphne: "Oh, Thelma, you're such a cunning linguist!"), and the rest of it pretty much writes itself. Sure, there are some potential pitfalls, like giving in to the urge to make the monsters real, or inexplicably including Batman, but for the most part the above formula works, which is why people stick to it. But oh, no; in addition to a ~~bunch herd flock~~ wrap of mummies *this* entry features a fight with a giant robot scorpion, the discovery of an honest-to-shit flying carpet (an event you'd think would challenge all their views on gravity, physics, and airline travel, but no one seems particularly impressed), and an encounter with some jokers who think Scooby-Doo is their reincarnated king. Okay, really, how many christing times are they going to trot out this cuntfucking "some faction thinks the resident goofball is their long-lost leader" bit? If you write cartoons for a living and you've ever used this idea, please, do children the world over a favor and kill yourself now. Because trust me, even to a five-year-old, you're a goddamned hack.

White Zombie

(1932)

Directed by Victor Halperin

The problem with zombies is that most of them are the "flesh-eating" variety and hardly any of them are the "sugarcane-harvesting" variety. They just don't know their place. Well, this is a pretty fossilized movie so these zombies aren't so uppity - dey's *all* workin' at de sugah mill! Of course, you get what you pay for - one zombie even falls into the goddamn sugar while they're grinding it up! I wouldn't buy that bag. Anyway, our story proper begins when this dude decides that he wants to poach another guy's wife. He hires the local voodoo MC to turn her into an old-school zombie, leaving her husband to assume she simply died, until, one day, he's informed otherwise. Here's his reaction:

HUSBAND: "Well surely you don't think she's alive, in the hands of natives? Oh *no*, better dead than that!"

Wow, complete fucking bigot much? The (racist) good guys decide to rescue the wife, which, to be honest, entails a lot of putzing around and not much else. Nothing really happens until the very end, when the voodoo master gets beaned on the noggin, prompting all his zombies to stroll right off a cliff. Just like those crazy lemmings, right Uncle Disney? The only good parts are a hottie in her underwear (1930's style), and the zombies tossing a butler into the moat. Zombies vs. butlers. Talk about your intra-class warfare.

Wicked Little Things

(2006)

Directed by J.S. Cardone

Do you know what happens if you don't buy enough life insurance? When you die, your wife and kids will be forced to relocate to a ramshackle hovel in the Pennsylvania mountains, where they'll be repeatedly ass-raped by Allstate spokesprick Dennis Haysbert. Oh, wait, that's what happens if you *do* buy the insurance. If you don't, your loved ones will still end up in the hovel, except now they'll be haunted by zombies. The zombies in question were once children who died in a mining accident (I guess that makes them a bunch of minor miners. Ha ha!), and since small children only have two settings – creepy and annoying – it's legitimately unsettling when they go on the rampage and start killing everyone they can get their tiny little hands on. It's all fairly spooky, there is some gore, and the mom and her teenaged daughter are both reasonably hot. (Oh, and there's a younger daughter too, for you Gary Glitter types.) Missteps include a little zombie girl suddenly breaking out the mad ninja throwing skills, and the huge spider the mom runs into in the woods, which must be a zombie itself to be successfully toughing it out through a Pennsylvania winter. I'm not gonna take this movie to task for niggardly little shit like that though, because I could never hate a movie that includes a conversation like this:

MOM: "Was it you who put the blood on our door?"

WEIRD MOUNTAIN GUY: "No need to thank me."

That's great.

Woke Up Dead

(2009)

Directed by Tim O'Donnell

Poor Napoleon Dynamite, forever cursed to play, well, Napoleon Dynamite. Let's face it, it's not like they're gonna hit this guy up to play King Lear or something. King Queer maybe. Anyway, in this zombie comedy (cue groans, items hurled at the television), he wakes up one day as, well, somebody's idea of a zombie, I guess. I mean, he's jonesing for brains, but he also develops infrared vision like Marvel Comics' Deathlok, healing powers like Marvel Comics' Wolverine, and super speed like Marvel Comics' Quicksilver. Maybe he's a zuvembie. So what does he do with his amazing new abilities? Why, he applies for an office job, so that tiresome workplace antics can ensue! Eventually we learn that there is, in fact, a longstanding conspiracy involving other zuvembies, but when Napoleon meets one of them they just use their powers to go on a penny-ante crime spree. It's less a zombie movie and more a cross between Bentley Little's bizarro novel *The Ignored* (1997) and the office comedy *Mandatory Overtime* (2006), and how's that for references so obscure they don't tell you squat? There's an *Iceman/Dinosaurus!* gag (how often do you hear one of those?), Newman from *Seinfeld* as the same fat fuck he always plays, a clip from *Zombie Nightmare* (1987), some cute tail (but no nudity), and Napoleon pukes a lot. Oh, and as a final middle finger to the audience, just as they're about to explain everything, the movie ends and the credits roll. Well fuck you, too, *Woke Up Dead*. **Fuck you too.**

Zombie 4: After Death

(1989)

Directed by Clyde Anderson

Several people are stranded an island overrun with zombies. Faces are torn off, heads explode, blood spews everywhere, and in one part a chick pulls her own eye out. There's no story or any boring shit like that.

Zombie 5: Killing Birds

(1987)

Directed by Claudio Lattanzi

That's right, *Zombie 5* was made **before** *Zombie 4*. Such is the insanity of foreign zombie movies. The trouble begins when this guy returns from the 'Nam to find his ol' lady *schtupping* another dude. He kills them both, plus her parents for good measure, then gets his EC Comics comeuppance when his wife's many pet birds blind him and pull one of his eyeballs out. Years later these college students who are majoring in Birds show up at the 'Nam guy's former pad looking for a rare woodpecker or something, and that night the place is besieged by zombies jonesing to kill them. The students who die are mostly guys, or chicks with fat asses, so the only real tragedy is when the sole hottie is dragged to her death through the rear window of their van. Eventually the survivors barricade themselves inside the house, but the zombies have seen that movie and just smash their way in through the walls. In the end only two birdophiles remain, and when they venture out the next morning the zombies are gone, and waiting for them is the blind, homicidal 'Nam vet, who's immediately killed by another flock of birds. Dumb story, medium gore, the hottie never gets naked. Pretty weak.

Zombie Apocalypse

(2011)

Directed by Nick Lyon

A chick once asked me just how many zombie movies there were, and when I told her, her next question was "Why?" It's a good question actually, because really, there's only so much you can do with the basic premise and all the endless variations – fast zombies, funny zombies, romantic zombies, hipster zombies – just nudge it further and further away from what made it work in the first place. That's why it's nice to see a simple, no-nonsense zombie movie like this one, where people are merely trying to get from point A to point B, and being thwarted by zombies. There's plenty of violence, the zombies look really good, there's a zombie dog, and they neatly sidestep the whole slow zombies vs. fast zombies issue by including both, wisely avoiding taking sides in one of the great dividing nerd debates of our time, easily surpassing Marvel vs. DC, Kirk vs. Picard, Joel vs. Mike, and Buffy the Vampire Slayer vs. Buffy the Vampire Slayer from behind. I wasn't too keen on the goony-ass thrilling climax (I mean, I guess there's no reason why one of those *couldn't* become a zombie, but... really?), but other than that this is a worthy, kickass zombie flick.

Zombie Bloodbath

(1993)

Directed by Todd Shits

Jesus all-you-can-eat Christ, I've never seen so many fat chicks in one movie before. They must've been busing them in for weeks. Anyway, it seems there was an accident at this nuclear power plant, so they abandoned it, knocked most of it down, and built a housing development right on top of the gutted remains. Seriously, they did everything but name the place "Love Canal Phase II". Now, you'd think this is something that would occasionally be mentioned by the local media, or at the very least become a part of neighborhood folklore, but somehow only one teenaged girl has even heard about it so it's a big joke on everyone when a bunch of zombies pop out of an old access tunnel and start devouring the white trash locals. The zombies quickly decimate the provincial dating pool, wiping out the resident girl gang *and* the broad who turns tricks down at the self-storage lot, prompting the locals to descend into the bowels of the abandoned power plant (played, unconvincingly, by the local Rotary Club) to kick some undead ass. As it turns out though, they're the ones who get their asses kicked, and before long gallons of blood, buckets of guts, and handfuls of mullet are littering the countryside. The gore's pretty fake but at least there's a lot of it, and if I was having a slow week I'd probably bang the clued-in teenage girl. Too bad she never gets naked.

Zombie Bloodbath 2

(1995)

Directed by Todd Shits

Okay, I cut the first *Zombie Bloodbath* a lot of slack, but making a Part 2 was going entirely too far. It starts with some convicts escaping from a hilariously fake "correctional institution" (I'm pretty sure they made the sign by cutting letters out of construction paper), while the kind of heavy metal people stopped listening to in 1988 plays. The convicts end up at this farmhouse where they cross paths with several "college students" (I'm assuming they're supposed to be the kind who go back to school after some time away, like say a decade) before they're all attacked by a satanic scarecrow and his army of zombies, who rise from their graves wearing Lakers gear and Stone Temple Pilots t-shirts. I guess this particular zombie master does all his recruiting at the pauper's cemetery. Almost every line of dialogue is hilariously retarded (like when the warden tells this guy that one of the prisoners was in for "mostly petty stuff", like bank robberies and murdering children), the plot twists are moronic beyond belief (like when they just happen to find several vials of flesh-eating bacteria in the front seat of a pickup truck), and, once again, it's stacked to the rafters with fat chicks. In fact, the only bim in this entire movie who looks like she could even spell "salad" is the girl I've dubbed "Yellow-Top Jersey-Hair". (Rest assured, you'll know her when you see her.) Yeah, I'd definitely hit that. But I wouldn't, you know, brag about it or anything.

Zombie Bloodbath 3: Undead Armageddon

(2000)

Directed by Todd Shits

If there's one thing Todd Shits (seriously, that's the name of the guy who makes these *Zombie Bloodbath* flicks: "Todd Shits") loves more than zombies, it's fat chicks. Either that or fat chicks are all that's available to him, in which case I really need to find out where these movies are made so I know never to go there. This one pits zombies from the future against high school kids serving detention, so it's kind of like *Night of the Living Dead* meets *The Breakfast Club* by way of *The Terminator*, assuming of course that all of those movies sucked an enormous amount of ass. And what the *hell* is that rumbling noise we hear every few seconds? It sounds like someone's bowling on the goddamned roof. Maybe it's supposed to be thunder. Or – and in my opinion this is a much more likely scenario – maybe the sound guy kept dropping their microphone down the stairs. As hard as it is to believe, this is actually *worse* than the previous *Zombie Bloodbath* movie; at least that one treated us to a gratuitous, full-on shot of Yellow-Top Jersey-Hair's crotch. Yeah, she had shorts on, but that just gives us all an opportunity to use our *imaginations*. In my imagination, for example, she had it shaved into the shape of Jon Bon Jovi's face. Anyway, forget about that; this movie fucking sucks. How they got permission to use the hit song "(I Just) Died in Your Arms Tonight" by Cutting Crew in such an disreputable pile, I'll never know.

Or... maybe they didn't.

Holy shit, if anyone from Virgin Records is reading this, it's about fifteen, sixteen minutes in. Please, please consider seizing and destroying every single copy of this movie. You'll be doing the world a favor, believe me.

The Zombie Chronicles

(2001)

Directed by Brad Sykes

Okay, *The Zombie Chronicles*, two stories does not an anthology movie make. Two stories just means you made two movies that you didn't feel like finishing. And no, the framing story doesn't count, especially when it's just some chick reporter (aside: she's fully bangable) endlessly chit-chatting with a weirdo until she's finally eaten by zombies for no discernible reason. Given the obvious level of dedication here, it should come as no surprise that our two feature stories are pretty slight too. In one, a zombie takes revenge on the people who took revenge on the army sergeant who killed him (yeah, it didn't make any sense to me either), and in the other, two guys and a girl camping near a cowboy graveyard earn the murderous ire of a zombie cowboy. (In the zombie cowboy's defense, I should probably mention that one of the guys did piss on his grave.) If you must watch this, don't miss the part where two grown men are knocked unconscious after running into each other, full-on Saturday morning cartoon style, and be sure to show some love for the female camper, because she's a real looker. It's a shame a zombie peels her adorable little face off - that was one of her two best features. The other being her rockin' bod, of course.

Zombie Cop

(1991)

Directed by J.R. Bookwalter

In the tradition of of *Maniac Cop* (1988), *Psycho Cop* (1989), *Demon Cop* (1991), and *Kid Cop* (1996) (okay, maybe not that last one), here's *Zombie Cop*, AKA a guy with his head wrapped in bandages. But that's positively epic compared to the costume his diabolical nemesis came up with: a Hawaiian shirt. Zombie Cop chases Hawaiian Shirt around for a while, until Hawaiian Shirt plummets over a seven-foot "cliff " and is impaled on a tree stump. The end. According to the credits, this movie was made in "Medina County, Ohio", and it looks like the kind of movie that would be made by people who live in a place called "Medina County, Ohio." It's a worthless piece of shit. Oh, and according to the video box it's ninety minutes long, but it really only clocks in at about an hour. Normally I hate it when home video packaging lies to me ("Robin Williams is delightful!"), but seeing as the result was thirty minutes less of *Zombie Cop*, this time I'm gonna count it in the movie's favor.

Zombieland

(2009)

Directed by Rubin Fleischer

Welcome to the most overrated zombie movie ever made that isn't *Day of the Dead* (1985). Hell, if you ask me this barely even qualifies as a zombie movie; it plays more like a road trip movie, with a few zombies thrown in for color. The jokes are embarrassingly predictable and think they're a lot funnier than they really are (Ha ha! He just wants a Twinkie! Fucking weak.); the whole "rules" angle is straight out of the book *The Zombie Survival Guide*; having characters physically interact with the credits and title is already beyond tiresome; and taking an extended break from the story to deep-throat Bill Murray's cock for several minutes was an inexcusably bad idea. Oh, and the payoff to the whole Bill Murray bit is so fucking stupid and obvious that the only reason "It's as obvious as the payoff to the Bill Murray scene in *Zombieland*" isn't already a common aphorism is because, frankly, it's kind of a mouthful. And then there's the imbecilic climax. Why does that amusement park still have power? Who's operating the rides if both girls are riding them? How could they *possibly* forget that all that light and noise would attract a messload of zombies? Did anyone use their brain *at all* when they came up with this scenario? Some bits do work, like when the two main guys are discussing the best zombie kills they've ever seen, but then they go and ruin the whole gag by bringing it up again and again and having the words "Zombie Kill of the Week" pop up on the screen in huge gold letters. I'm not fucking retarded, okay? You don't have to duct tape how clever you are to a sledgehammer and beat me over the fucking head with it. I wouldn't go so far as to say that this a movie made for condescending tourists who hate exactly this type of movie – it's not Wes Craven's *Scream* (1996) – but it's definitely scalping tickets outside the same ballpark. Fuck you, *Zombieland*. You can suck my huge.

Zombie Nation

(2006)

Directed by Ulli Lommel

"From the director of *The Boogeyman*" proclaims the DVD case. That would be the 1980 movie *The Boogeyman*, and that's not such a bad credential. Not mentioned, however, is the fact that this guy was also responsible for *Boogeyman II* (1982), *Return of the Boogeyman* (1994), and *Boogeyman 2: Redux* (2003), all of which were complete fucking hose jobs. And you might as well add *Zombie Nation* to that second list, because this flick is a complete waste of time. Our main guy, a cop by day and also a serial killer by day, works for the most budget-strapped police force I've ever seen: they don't own a single proper patrol car, and their precinct is obviously located in an old warehouse that doubles as storage for someone's klieg lights. And what is with the prominently-placed gong? Did someone see that in the prop room and say "Hey, let's put this gong in there. That's something that would be in a police station, right? A gong?" Anyway, our killer cop's *modus operandi* is pretty simple: pull chicks over, handcuff them, drag them home, and finish them off in time to watch *Mass for Shut-Ins*. His stupefyingly clueless partner ("What are we doing with that big heavy duffel bag in the back?") lets him get away with it at first, but eventually he starts to squawk, at which point the rest of the force quickly takes action... by instigating a cover-up that includes planting evidence, framing an innocent man, and even home-invading the snitch's house and beating him shitless right in front of his wife! Fucking cops - anything, *anything* to avoid paperwork. Fortunately, while the system may fail, we still have black magic: it seems one of the murdered girls was under a voodoo spell of protection, and while it obliviously didn't work very well (lawsuit) it does allow *all* of the killer's victims to rise from the dead as yummy female zombies. And I'm not going all necro when I say they're yummy, because their zombie makeup consists *entirely* of some black stuff smeared around the eyes. You'd get the same result pushing an emo chick into the pool. The denouement? ("Denouement" is French for "let's get this over with".) Our undead lovelies track the evil cop down and eat him. Proving, if nothing else, that none of them are Jewish. Ha ha! Get it? Because... oh, never mind.

Zombies' Lake

(1981)

Directed by J. A. Laser

We open with a delicious hottie stripping, sunbathing, swimming, and then, completely out of solo activities that begin with the letter S, being attacked by a zombie. Her full-frontal will be sorely missed. And it seems this sexy tragedy could have been prevented: the fact that the lake is haunted by dead Nazis is common knowledge in the nearby village, as made clear during the endless, boring World War Part 2 flashback the mayor sets up. After the Nazi zombies claim several more victims – including most of a woman's basketball team, while they're naked (the girls are naked, I mean, not the zombies) – the mayor asks for some outside assistance, only to end up with a pair of big-city dicks who treat the villagers like hopeless rubes. ("Let's split, " says one of these guys. "Let's get away from this heap of hicks.") Eventually the zombies raid the village in broad daylight, trashing the pub and killing every topless chick they see. Subjugating Europe was one thing, but these Nazis have gone entirely too far, so the locals finally step up and nuke their undead asses with a flamethrower. Minimal blood, but lots of tits and full-frontal, and I gotta give 'em props for actually putting their titular plural-possessive apostrophe in the proper place. It's a detail most people would've gotten wrong. Because you're all fucking illiterate.

Zombies of Mora Tau

(1957)

Directed by Edward Cahn

Seems Africa has quite the zombie infestation, not that they let it bother them; when a zombie jaywalks, for example, they just run that sucker down and go about their business. Maybe this is because the zombies' only real sore spot is the sunken treasure ship full of diamonds located nearby, which explains why they up their game considerably when some divers arrive to salvage the thing. The zombies make it a point to go after these cats, and, now that they're properly motivated, they even take the time to kidnap this racktacular brunette and turn *her* into a zombie. (I gotta say, zombified or not, I'd definitely bury my face in *that* pair. They are un-fucking-believable.) Zombie chick's finest moment: a guy she's closing in on bounces a candlestick right off her forehead, and she doesn't even flinch. Now that's acting. In the end the divers manage to salvage the diamonds anyway, only to learn that the zombies are just gonna keep on coming unless they destroy the treasure forever. So they half-heartedly toss the diamonds back into the sea – from the beach, mind you – and the zombies immediately vanish. Okay, what? Seriously, a five-year-old could wade out there and collect that ice now! You're really telling me that after all the fucking grief they put everyone through, these diamond-hoarding, stingy-ass zombie Jews are perfectly okay with this non-solution? What the fuck? Zombies are idiots.

Zombies Unleashed

(2010)

Directed by Richard Lee Givens

Welp, I see the zombies got Darlene Connor. I was always a Becky man myself.

We open with a calculatedly multicultural crew (black guy, Hispanic guy, white dork, woman) cruising the streets, performing drive-bys on zombies and pondering why the undead bastards have taken to attacking each other. But is this a full-blown zombie apocalypse, or just a localized inconvenience? Damned if I know - zombies and looters seem to be an ever-present concern, but at the same time all the stores are still open. (Sorry, but if you expect me to come in during the zombie apocalypse, I better be getting *at least* time-and-a-half.) In fact, most of this movie makes zero sense. I mean, the public is clearly aware that there's a zombie epidemic, but nobody seems particularly concerned, and even the members of our main crew, who consider themselves an "elite zombie hit squad", have no qualms about taking a group nap in their car with the windows rolled down. There's no discernible story, the "zombies attacking each other" angle is never explored, I'd hardly call it gory, and there are entirely too many instances of chicks peeing (sorry, Richard Lee Givens, that's really not my thing). In the end, the sole highlight is a sexy stripper who never even finishes stripping. And I think we can all agree that that's just not right.

Zombiethon

(1986)

Directed by Ken Dixon

Okay, this isn't a real zombie movie, as such, it's just several scenes from other zombie movies all strung together, kind of like a zombie highlight reel except compiled at a time when there were only 30 or so zombie movies to choose from and 23 of them refused to participate. There's the zombie vs. shark and eyeball vs. splinter scenes from *Zombie* (1979), assorted zombies chowing down on people, lots of tits and full-frontal, and women sexually assaulted by an invisible monkey. You may question how that last one fits, but think about it - if you had access to footage of chicks being sexually assaulted by an invisible monkey, wouldn't you break it out every chance you got? If you like zombie movies but don't have time for all that boring characterization and plot, this and *Zombie 4: After Death* are probably you two best bets.

Special shout-out to the brunette in the schoolgirl outfit: If you weren't currently 27 years order than you are in this video, I would so fuck you.

Zombie Town

(2007)

Directed by Damon Lemay

This opens with zombie patient zero's first victim tearing into some rednecks, followed by the credits, which are backed by heavy metal music. Why must these cheap zombie movies always feature heavy metal soundtracks? It's the 21st century for fuck's sake, who the dick listens to heavy metal anymore? Trust me, nouveau heavy metal bands, you sound like assholes. Please, send your royalty check to Iron Maiden and shut the fuck up already. Fortunately, once we're past the credits this flick picks up considerably, and it categorically earns my mid-level recommendation: the characters behave like real people; the main chick is a hot redhead; there's some great, over-the-top gore; and we're graced with one scrumptious pair of tits. I didn't appreciate the annoying dick who was there solely to say tasteless shit and sport *That '70s Show* style sideburns, nor did I care for the heroes' little plan at the end, which was poorly thought-out and resulted in the squandering of a perfectly doable blonde. But it was nice to see the action range all over the hick burg where this movie was shot; I'm so tired of zombie flicks that take place entirely in the woods, or in one lousy hood. It looks like everyone in town really got behind these filmmakers and their dream to make a gory, repulsive sci-fi/horror movie. And it the end, isn't that what America is all about? Little pink houses for you and me.

Zomblies

(2010)

Directed by David M. Reynolds

Chinese stereotype? ("Rook out! Zomblies cloming!") Typo? Maybe it's supposed to be pronounced "Zomb-LIES", you know, like lies about zombies. (Example: "We really needed another movie where military guys fight zombies in the woods!") Anyway, it's a stupid, clumsy title, heralding the same old shit, although the action does eventually move into a few abandoned buildings that the director swears we have permission to shoot in but if the cops show up, run. The only notable deviation from formula is that this movie features both slow *and* fast zombies, and the fast ones are apparently preying on the slow. It's an interesting sociological and/or evolutionary development, so naturally this movie does nothing with it; even the "advanced" fast zombies aren't smart enough to do much more than bum-rush every food source they see. I think we need to accept the fact that, with a few exceptions, zombies are never going to be able to master any tool more complicated than a machete, a club, or possibly Microsoft Paint. To be fair, *Zomblies* does look reasonably slick and professional, but it's all just so tiresome, and at approximately half the length of a "real" movie it still feels too damn long, although this was probably exasperated by the fact that I watched it on cuntfucking YouTube, which always takes forever since YouTube videos no longer pre-load and end up freezing over and over again until you're so furious that you put your fist through your laptop and then have to drive to the store to buy another one, bringing the total running time of this movie to nearly four hours, depending on traffic. Seriously, YouTube, your job is to play videos. If you can't handle that anymore, do us all a favor and stop existing.

Don't miss out!

Visit the website below and you can sign up to receive emails whenever Mr. Satanism publishes a new book. There's no charge and no obligation.

https://books2read.com/r/B-A-TCXC-KBLJ

BOOKS 2 READ

Connecting independent readers to independent writers.

Also by Mr. Satanism

66.6 Absurd Movies About the Devil
Legendary House of Haunted Hell
Trash of the Titans
Night of the Living Dud
Lifetime Movies... for Men
Shark Weak: The Worst Shark Movies Ever Made
The Not-At-All-Cleverly-Titled Book of Dragon Movies
Snakes, Rats, Spiders, and Bats: A Creepy-Crawly Movie
Compendium
Monkeys & Dinosaurs: Cinema as High Art, Vol. 1
Hex Crimes: The Worst Witch Movies Ever Made
Close Encounters of the Worst Kind
Triskaidekaphilia - Mr. Satanism's 13th Book
Vampire Movies Suck
Werewolves Don't Eat Brunch
Mr. Satanism's Invisible Book
A Yeti Brew (And Bigfoot Too)
The Magical Golden Rainbow Book of Crappy Wizard of Oz
Movies
Cannibal Attraction
A Chronology on Elm Street
Mr. Satanism Puts Down Your Favorite Dog (...Movies)
A Collection of Woke Movie Reviews